ACCESS TO THE AMERICAN MIND

The Impact of the
New Mass Media

ACCESS TO THE AMERICAN MIND

The Impact of the New Mass Media

Martin H. Seiden, Ph.D.

SHAPOLSKY PUBLISHERS, INC., NEW YORK

A Shapolsky Book

For any additional information, contact:
Shapolsky Publishers, Inc.
136 West 22nd Street
New York, NY 10011
(212) 633-2022

1 2 3 4 5 6 7 8 9 10

Library of Congress Cataloging-in-Publication Data
Seiden, Martin, H., 19–
Access to the American mind : the impact of
the new mass media / Martin H. Seiden
p.   cm.
Includes bibliographical references
ISBN 0-944007-71-6
1. Mass media—United States.   I. Title.
P92.U5S45   1991
302.23′0973—dc20   90-47617

Design and Typography by The Bartlett Press, Inc.
Somerset, New Jersey

Printed and bound by Graficromo s.a., Cordoba, Spain

To my wife, Rosalie,
and to my wonderful children, Shoshana and Amos

We do not err because truth is
difficult to see. It is visible
at a glance. We err because it
is more comfortable.
—Aleksandr Solzhenitsyn

Contents

Introduction

There is a standard approach to books written on the subject of mass communications. Almost without exception, they try to show that the owners of the mass media and advertisers who use the mass media psychologically rape an innocent and naive public.

On the front of the dust jacket of a typical recent media book was written in bold print: A STARTLING REPORT ON THE 50 CORPORATIONS THAT CONTROL WHAT AMERICA SEES, HEARS, AND READS.[1] On the back of the jacket Ralph Nader claims that the author is "the conscience of American journalism." The book was written by a Pulitzer Prize–winning journalist who was an editor of one of America's major dailies and is now on the faculty of the School of Journalism of a major university. Credentials beyond reproach.

In any library one will find a shelf of similar books, half of which eagerly reveal that the media are controlled by a small group of men who are up to no good. The other half of the shelf offers books that reveal how these men manipulate the public. This type of exposé literature caters to the intellectuals' paranoia and belief in conspiracy theories. Such books are assured publication and invariably receive favorable reviews. Publishers generally have several such titles on their list. This despite the fact that most authors include publishers on their list of evildoers.

One is expected to believe that America's communications system is owned and used by greedy and grubby businessmen who will go to any length and are prepared to commit any evil in order to sell soap. Because the boards of directors of all corporations, including media corporations, consist of executives of *other* corporations, it is assumed that they protect one another from having their respective nefarious activities exposed. It is further expected that you not only believe in their willingness to be evil but that you believe that they can, in fact, implement their evil designs—that the modern system of mass communications uniquely affords them that opportunity!

Certainly there are people who will commit crimes for far less than the numbers that will appear on the corporation's next quarterly statement. But this "communications literature" expects you to believe that anti-social behavior is in fact necessary in order to accomplish most commercial objectives.

Not only are most of the allegations in this type of literature untrue—as we shall see from the contents of this book—but this view of the mass media is harmful. It directs our attention away from the real sources of social and political problems and focuses the blame on the owners and users of electronic hardware.

The book referred to at the opening of this discussion makes the following statement on page 47:

> The deeper social loss of giantism in the media is not in its unfair advantage in profits and power. This is real and it is serious. But the gravest loss is in the self-serving censorship of political and social ideas, in news, magazine articles, books, broadcasting and movies. Some intervention by owners is direct and blunt. But most of the screening is subtle, some not even occurring at the conscious level, as when subordinates learn by habit to conform to the owners'

ideas. But subtle or not, the ultimate result is a distorted reality and impoverished ideas.

Having said this, the author, who is in the front rank of American journalism, says, unembarrassed, the following, just two pages later: "So it is ironic that in the last decade the most bitter attacks on the media have come from the American corporate system."

Perhaps the hostility to which he refers is an indication that the owners and directors of American corporations do *not* control the media? The Pulitzer Prize–winning author also fails to explain how "giantism" failed to save such former giants as the *New York Herald Tribune, Saturday Evening Post, Life*, RCA, the radio networks, and the major movie studios, just to mention a few of the powerful who have faded from the scene.

He goes on to attack corporate America for the evils of "poisoning our drinking water, food and in some cases whole communities." These accusations are not shocking, for we have heard, read, and seen them before. Where? In the same mass media owned by a corporate America. So where is this conspiracy of power?

The intellectuals' perception of how the mass media function is all too often based on *a priori* reasoning, supported by hoary examples and anecdotes. This book challenges these allegations. The present author tries to bring the reader into the inner workings of the mass communications system, to show how decisions are really made and how the media go about trying to achieve their objectives of informing, entertaining, and selling. And, finally, this author will try to shed light on the misconceptions inherent in the cliché "power of the media"—a cliché that reflects ignorance of the process of the formation and transmission of ideas.

The book quoted above that has served as an example of typical media literature reflects a phenomenon that has taken hold of America in the past half-century: America is today in the iron grip of an unthinking intellectual elite; the high priests of this

elite are not Nobel Prize winners but journalists who generally
do not confine themselves to their principal purpose, which is
the collection and transmission of information. More frequently
than not, they set themselves up as judge and jury on whatever
the subject may be. And they have the unique opportunity of
publicizing their views. They swarm over an issue like articulate
locusts, mindlessly devouring the subject, and then move on,
ignoring the devastation they leave behind.

As we approach the end of the twentieth century we find that
journalists' "sacred cows" include South Africa, the Palestinians,
women's rights, abortion, AIDS, and the evils of corporations,
of cholesterol, of fur coats, of atomic energy and of chemicals
of all sorts (except drugs). This list will change with time. The
main characteristic of these *causes* is that they are not heard of
again once they are dropped from the intellectuals' list of good
and evil. But while they are held to be sacred, they are universal
and unquestioned.

Most of those who endorse the latest causes feel that by doing
so they are projecting an image of intellectuality and moral
sensitivity. But they fail at both because few study the issues that
underlie their adopted convictions. Why investigate, when one
would not dare to express an alternative point of view while these
issues are held to be sacred?

We hear so much about South Africa but virtually nothing regarding the condition of the average black elsewhere in Africa.
Nor has anyone reported on discrimination against whites in independent Africa. One hears a great deal about the "occupied
territories" in Israel but nothing regarding the "occupied territories" in the center of American cities that Americans dare not
enter at night.

We do not hear from journalists, columnists, program producers, or talk-show hosts regarding the effects on children of being
raised by working mothers, or the emotional after-effects of abortion, or the tragedy of innocent heterosexual victims of AIDS.
When have we heard Vietnamese refugees explain why they are

throwing themselves at the mercy of the South China Sea? Vietnam is an old sacred cow about which we hear no more; the subject has been ravaged and the intellectuals have since moved on to more up-to-date causes.

It is difficult to find a journalist who will risk his or her reputation by going against the profession's moral position on these matters. Our public debates are kept on the straight and narrow. As we shall show in this book, the power of the media is really the power of the journalists to push *their* latest cause. Sophisticated technological hardware doesn't necessarily assure sophisticated thinking or objective information.

The real corporate conspiracy would appear to be the corporations' bond of uncritical silence regarding the operation of their media. Corporate executives appear to be paralyzed by the fear of being devoured by the mindless swarm if they interfere. What sensible executive would jeopardize his company's profit-and-loss statement by triggering a strike because he took issue with one of the journalists' sacred causes?

It is unlikely that this book will find favor with the fraternity that must pass judgment on it: the professional press. But if it succeeds in opening the door to a more balanced consideration of the issues of the day, the author will have succeeded, nevertheless.

Power of the Media

The Messengers

A torrent of information, advertising, and entertainment pours through the 1,700 daily newspapers, 10,500 AM and FM radio stations, 1,400 commercial and educational television stations, and 8,000 cable television systems serving the American audience. In addition to this formidable array of facilities that provide daily service, there are in the United States 7,800 *weekly* newspapers and over 9,600 weekly, monthly, and quarterly magazines and journals.

Only with the greatest difficulty can anyone in the United States avoid the mass media. Indeed, the average American is exposed to the messages of these media to a far greater extent than to formal education, organized religion, or political parties.

There seems to be a consensus that this extensive exposure to the mass media places it high on the list of social institutions that affect human behavior. One popular theory has gone so far as to assert that "the medium is the message," that it is the means rather than the content of communications that influences

1

the audience.[1] The fact that such a notion is taken seriously reveals the strength of the underlying conviction—that there is something *intrinsically* powerful about mass communications. This implies a belief that the human psyche is malleable and that with the right formula or even simply with sufficient exposure to the media, audiences can be manipulated. Indeed, not only is this view encouraged by advertising agencies but also by a new profession of "media men" that has evolved in recent years whose purpose is the sale and merchandising of political candidates through the "proper" use of the mass media.

It is understandable in the light of these beliefs that the mass media are for many a source of anxiety, and for some a source of fear. This explains why the mass media are held responsible for so many of our social, political, and even physical ills. Thus, political leaders blame the media when their popularity wanes, and as we shall see, the media are believed to bear a large part of the responsibility for the growth of crime in America's cities, for social unrest, narcotics addiction, children's reading disabilities, and even for lung cancer and heart disease.

Consider what has taken place in recent years: how Americans work and relax, our view of morality and ethics and our sense of aesthetics. These have all undergone revolutionary change in the very brief period of 15 or 20 years. What would have been met with shock, opprobrium, or even a prison sentence is not only socially acceptable, but is now a civil right. This includes burning the American flag, performing and undergoing an abortion, homosexual "marriages," spreading a fatal disease such as AIDS, and performing bodily functions on prime-time television. Today, schoolgirls live in coed dorms, women serve on American warships and train with men at the same boot camps.

On the other hand, behavior that was once considered a part of the wholesome life has become a crime. This includes smoking in public places, prayer in the nation's schools, maintaining a private club for selected members, special treatment for women in the workforce, and censoring public entertainment.

While social norms were undergoing a revolution, another one was taking place in communications. We were plugging ourselves into myriad new technological equipment that included—in addition to the familiar television and radio stations—personal computers, Walkmans, cable television, satellite television, VCRs, compact discs, and fax machines.

Is there a connection? Did the mass media deliver the "message"? Are they responsible for the attitudinal changes? Are those who own or those who operate the electronic media exerting an influence on society? Has the drive to sell commercial products fostered an irresponsible pandering that has transformed our sense of values? Or are none of these true? Do the changes come from another source? Is there another way of gaining access to the American mind than through the mass media?

An answer to these important issues calls for an understanding of the way in which the mass media operate. Only then can we come to conclusions regarding the responsibility of the media for the earth-shaking changes that are taking place in America's values and mores.

Unfortunately, the inner workings of mass communications in America are not generally understood. The author has found that even those directly involved—members of the government's regulatory staff and employees of the media themselves—lack a clear picture of the system's more important aspects. Each knows the workings of his own sphere but has only the vaguest notion of how the rest of the system operates. Those in advertising only vaguely comprehend the use of satellites. Few newspaper people know about microwave interconnection and fiber optics. Most program syndicators don't know what the Federal Communications Commission (FCC) license renewal process involves. The FCC staff has almost no knowledge of how time buyers operate, and few television program producers understand the strategy of newspaper or magazine editing. Least informed of all, however, are the so-called opinion makers—the nation's political leaders, writers, and intellectuals. We will look into the inner workings of the system later in our discussion. First, let us have a look at what has been going on in the absence of this information.

Protecting the American Mind

There was a time not too long ago when concern for the audience set in motion pressure for greater regulation. The forces of the government were marshalled to contain, if not to subdue, the allegedly powerful media.

Fear of the media, particularly television, runs deep. There have, in the past, been a number of attempts to confine the media's area of activity and to create countervailing forces to its freedom of action.

Thus, the government has studied the impact on our young people of the violence shown on television. Congress banned the broadcasting of cigarette commercials and investigated the relationship between the advertising of drugs and our narcotics problem; the courts required broadcasters to accept *anti*-commercials. In the past the Justice Department filed suit to break up the television networks, while the White House once called for greater control by local television broadcasters over network news. The FCC has limited the prime-time programming of the television networks to three of the four prime-time hours (7–11 P.M.). At the same time, broadcast licenses are periodically threatened by federal attempts to restructure the industry so that it will conform to the government's definition of socially responsible behavior.

All these acts—and we could point to many more—reflect the fear and hostility felt in some quarters toward the mass media. This hostility even spilled over to those who serve in its front ranks: Journalists have from time to time been the subject of court orders, and a few have actually gone to jail for failure to reveal their sources of information or for publishing "stolen" information, as the Supreme Court stripped the journalist of his traditional immunity.[2]

Then something very strange occurred. The administration of President Ronald Reagan altered the government's direction. It actively sought to lower the government's profile, particularly its regulatory profile. Deregulation became public policy. At about the same time, the liberal and the intellectual communities—which loathed the Reagan Administration—rallied to the support of an "anti Reagan" Supreme Court as the court adopted a radically new policy. It saw the Constitution as guaranteeing *the right of privacy*.

Ironically, this new interpretation of the Constitution was in the spirit of deregulation. It banned public interference in broad areas of personal behavior. Under the new rules, for example, it became impossible to restrict pornography. This allowed the networks to engage in an unfettered use of the medium at the very time that they were engaged in a mortal conflict with new technology. (This new technology, as we shall see later, is cutting ever deeper into the programming monopoly held by the networks for so many years.) Now, protected from even a whisper of censorship, the networks moved ever deeper into what had until then been subjects and depictions that were at best questionable. Their objective: to hold on to their audiences at all cost!

All efforts by the liberal and intellectual communities to have the government exercise even indirect control over the programming of the mass media, for what they perceived to be to the benefit of the mass audience, were now abandoned. The extraordinary battle fought over the appointment of Robert Bork to the Supreme Court revealed the unusual turnabout that had taken place in the agenda of the opposing forces. The liberal and intellectual communities had surrendered their elitist philosophy and adopted the view that the government was not a tool for social control, except in the most extreme circumstances. A sense of social *laissez-faire* had overtaken the nation. Today no one wants to protect the American citizen from the powerful media.

Was the abandonment of the desire to exercise control over the mass media a defeat for the forces of good? Was the nation now at the mercy of the unscrupulous, the panderers, the manipulators?

Reality

To gain perspective over this emotionally charged issue, one must first remember that before the electronic media the public was served exclusively by newspapers, journals, and books. There was never the concern or desire for control or regulation of the printed media as there has been over television. The electronic media are feared because they are at the service of the masses in ways that the written word has never been. Those who read are considered more intelligent, more resistant to false messages, than the unwashed masses. Yet history has shown us that some of the most menacing ideas of the nineteenth and twentieth centuries have been the product of intellectuals. What, in fact, has been the record of television regarding the power of the dark forces over society?

Televised congressional hearings brought down Senator Mc-Carthy despite his reputation of being a demagogue. It forced a president of the United States to resign for the first time in American history. It helped to ease out of office a powerful Speaker of the House, and it exposed a multimillion-dollar plot to deal in arms and wage war—against the specific desire of Congress.

This is quite a record. And it all occurred despite the wealth and expertise at the disposal of those who appeared before the television audience. The evidence would tend to raise serious questions over whether the media are truly powerful in their ability to serve those who would hoodwink the public. Indeed, evidence tends to indicate that it is a tool that is serving the masses rather than those who operate it or appear on it.

A study that adds considerable support to this thesis was published by the U.S. Army in August 1989. It concluded that the media were not responsible for the loss of public support for the Vietnam War. The Army Center of Military History concluded that the press reports were more accurate than the public statements of the administration in portraying the situation in Vietnam—a confession that is of considerable significance, considering its source. William Hammond, who wrote the 413-page study entitled "The Military and the Media," has said: "In the end President Johnson and his advisers put too much faith in public relations. . . ." This was a nice way of saying that the public is not so easily manipulated.

The report says that "What alienated the American public in both the Korean and the Vietnam wars was not news coverage but casualties. . . ." Public support for each war dropped by 15 percentage points whenever U.S. casualties increased by a factor of 10. . . . Given the restrictions and limited goals that Johnson adopted, such as no extension of the ground war to North Vietnam, Cambodia or Laos for it might induce China to enter the war, the practical initiative rested with the enemy. . . . The enemy could withdraw into his sanctuaries to mend and regroup." In effect it was a no-win situation. Regarding the power of television, the Army's report goes on to say: "Critics of the media in the military misassessed the nature of television coverage which, despite isolated instances to the contrary, was banal and stylized."

Despite the foregoing confession of a military man, and years of experience in which powerful political figures have fallen before public scrutiny, rather than the reverse, there persists the fear that the audience can be manipulated through clever use of television. The nightmare is that a charismatic personality can buy his way to political power in ways that were not possible without television, and threaten the foundations of the republic. What, in fact, has been the experience of politicians?

The idea that with enough money the right media man can win public office for his client is inconsistent with the facts. A special study made in 1970 showed that in 14 out of 32 senatorial contests the winner spent *less* than the loser, and among the relatively big spenders who won, most were incumbents. Furthermore, a detailed description of the techniques employed by successful media men (see Chapter 5) reveal that it is the candidate who is influenced by the public and not the reverse. Neither heavy expenditures nor the wisest use of the mass media necessarily "molds" public opinion. More frequently than not, success follows from an accurate assessment of the public will.

What about the assumption that crime in the streets is somehow related to violence shown on television? The National Institute of Mental Health, the highly respected government research center, after spending much time and money investigating this allegation, could find no solid evidence linking the inordinate display of violent behavior shown on most children's television programs with the current high crime rate. It did not recommend controls over television.

These findings were similar to an earlier study on the role of comic books. Most important, they concur with the observed behavior of the vast majority of American youth. As we shall see in Chapter 8, young people—those who were raised with television and who at the time of the Vietnam War were in their teens and early twenties—were the group in America that was most outspoken in opposition to the violence in Vietnam. They were also in the vanguard in the early civil rights campaigns and were among the most active in opposing sexual discrimination. Paradoxically, those who were, at the time, over thirty were generally indifferent to the social and political problems of the period and were suitably dubbed by the president the "silent majority." The over-thirty group, however, was exposed in its youth to radio programs and movies relatively free of the violence so common in the mass media today.

This is not to say that violence is a desirable form of entertainment, but rather that there is substantial evidence that indicates that exposure to it or to any subject is not necessarily a form of instruction nor does it necessarily condition the audience, however young, in such a way as to offset or replace the more fundamental influences of family, friends, and school.

From the perspective of their day-to-day routine, one can observe that in the American system of mass communication *power*—defined as *control*—really resides with the audience and not with the media. The audience influences the type of entertainment, consumer products, and political programs that are brought before it by the mass media. And this is nowhere more pronounced than in television, the medium that has been considered the *most powerful* of these mass media.

As we shall explore in some detail, the democratic character of America's mass media is a natural outgrowth of economics. America's media system operates on the premise that the audience is the customer and that those who own and use the system are salesmen. This relationship permeates the entire system, affecting its financing, its content, and even the nature of political advocacy. By constantly being polled, the audience determines the type of programming that it is offered. Polls, as we shall see, also serve as a guide in the design of political platforms and even political policy. They are used to determine the type of products marketed through the media as well as their packaging, and even their name.

Because the audience's attention is so essential to the system, its influence is exercised in its day-to-day operation and not as a vague intangible desire to please on the part of the system's owners or operators.

That the mass media lack an *intrinsic* power to influence the public is clear if we consider those whom they would influence. The American audience is not a homogeneous mass. It consists of many sub-audiences. These include the different races, religions, and ethnic and national cultures in the United States, as well as individual differences in sex, age, education, wealth, and local origin.

Because of this diversity, the American audience lives by many different value systems. This provides for a wide range of reactions to the same information. What will attract one group will alienate another. The value systems that are unique to each sub-audience have deep cultural and historical roots. These are not communicated, they are inculcated. This is done by family, friends, and school, not by speeches, dramatizations, or 30-second "spot" announcements. However, like potholes in a poorly paved road, value systems generally leave some areas unfilled. In these areas, the media can have some effect on the attitude of an audience toward a subject that, for this audience, is of secondary importance. It is at this level that most commercial products seek to influence the public. This is the world in which advertisers operate.

But, for the same reason that the selection of a particular brand of soap, cereal, or toothpaste is a relatively unimportant matter for most people, it is also difficult to create a brand loyalty. A successful advertising campaign is one that succeeds in familiarizing the public with the product (strangers are seldom invited into one's home) and possibly in generating some curiosity about the product's effectiveness (*new, improved*, etc.). In effect, advertisers are pleaders, not manipulators. Their impact, when there is one, is short-lived.

Even if they wanted to, there is evidence that the mass media cannot alter or affect deep-rooted attitudes. The failure of anti-cigarette commercials on television and radio is a case in point. Even with a well-advertised threat of excruciating death and testimonials by dying victims, cigarette sales continued to increase until a new generation switched its preference to alcohol and drugs.

Another dramatic example of the ineffectiveness of the mass media in shaping our fundamental attitudes is the failure of wartime propaganda. How many people still bear hostile feelings toward the Germans and Japanese after five years of vituperation by the mass media during the Second World War? And with what ease have both the U.S. and China renounced their mutual suspicion of one another after decades of active hostility and—for China—decades of anti-American propaganda. The same can be said to apply to Eastern Europe and the U.S.S.R. Is this an indication of the ease with which public opinion is molded? Or is it not an indication that public opinion was never molded at all?

Or take the question of race relations. The complete absence of blacks from commercials, news programming, and dramatizations of everyday life was rectified in the 1970s. Their absence, of course, had been a form of information. It told them and the white audience a great deal about the accepted position of blacks (and other nonwhites) in our social structure. But the media were not responsible for the past repression. Nor should they now be credited with leading the nation into the new era of greater racial equality.

The changing role of the blacks in mass communications followed the civil rights upheaval of the 1960s. The black revolution in America and its acceptance by the white majority were not a product of mass communications, but of forces more fundamental to the formation of private and public attitudes. The causes lie much deeper than 30-second "spot" announcements or dramatizations on brotherhood. In racial matters, as elsewhere, the media merely acted as a mirror of society, not the molder of its opinions, as the cliché would have us believe.

Myths concerning the power of the media are a serious matter, for they are diverting us from identifying and coping with the real causes of difficult social and political problems.

The Government's Role

Under proper control, government can be an efficient provider of important social services. But without effective external control, its unbridled power becomes a public menace without parallel. The mass media, to the extent that they are independent of the government, are or should be the government's principal adversary and therefore its principal external control. The American Constitution, in its infinite wisdom, saw the press as an important countervailing force to government power and, through the First Amendment, in effect gave it an independence no less important than that of the Supreme Court.

Thus, to call upon the government to control the mass media is to subvert the principal control placed over the government. A free "press" is the linchpin of the American political system. If it had had its way, would the government have permitted such frank television reporting from Vietnam? Or would it have allowed the *Washington Post* to investigate and report on its findings in what later became known as the Watergate affair? These two issues alone raise serious questions regarding the effectiveness of the traditional checks and balances in our political system, for neither the Congress nor the judiciary was equal to the task. This indicates the enormous importance of a free media as a partner in government.

No less important in evaluating the government's future role as a regulator of the mass media is its terrible record as a source of reliable information. In the past, Americans had been accustomed to expect from their government a high degree of reliability in its official announcements. Occasional scandals yes, but not the *official* release of blatantly false information or the concealment of information to which the public has a right. Unhappily, this is not always the case.

Erik Barnouw, a leading historian of mass communication, calls attention to one such breach of the American tradition of free public access to information by the late Secretary of State John Foster Dulles. In Barnouw's book, *The Image Empire*, the author relates how, in August 1955, the communist regime of Mao Tsetung declared itself willing to admit American newsmen in return for the admission of Chinese newsmen into the United

States. Dulles refused. Indeed, so stringent was the ban on information from China that when, in defiance of the State Department, William Worthy, a reporter for the Baltimore *Afro-American*, went to China, Under Secretary of State Robert Murphy successfully prevailed on William Paley of CBS not to carry Worthy's shortwave news reports.[3]

For the next 15 years, the American people were compelled to rely on the State Department, itself poorly informed, for information relating to China. Our resulting ignorance of China had a good deal to do with the government's misreading of the situation in Vietnam. As the *New York Times* editorialized on the day before the cease-fire in Vietnam, "the United States might not have gone into Vietnam had the depth of the schism between the Soviet Union and China been clearly perceived."[4]

With increasing frequency, the federal government also adopted a policy of releasing information that was patently false. The Eisenhower Administration denied that U-2 over-flights ever took place until the Russians paraded Gary Powers, the U-2 pilot, before the world press. Similarly, the Kennedy Administration initially denied our involvement in the Bay of Pigs fiasco, and gave numerous contradictory responses for our involvement in Vietnam. And President Johnson provided the Congress with patently false information on the Gulf of Tonkin incident. Subsequent attempts to disguise military and political bungling became so blatant that the term "credibility gap," a euphemism for government lying, came into widespread use. Today, falsification and concealment of information have become commonplace in the executive branch of the government. "Watergate" and "Iran-gate" have become part of our political folklore.

For our purposes, two aspects of Watergate merit particular attention. First, the entire affair revolved around the attempt to control, create, and alter information. In the modern world the sum and substance of power rests on the public's ability or inability to obtain access to accurate information. The audacious manner in which the White House staff sought to monopolize political power by manipulating and stealing information was a natural outgrowth of the passivity with which the public and the Congress accepted the earlier concealment and falsification of information by the executive branch.

Watergate also underlined the importance of a privately controlled mass media. The initial revelations of the affair were not the work of the Justice Department or of any government agency, but of two staffers on the *Washington Post*. And unlike most congressional hearings that go unpublicized, the mass media, particularly television, recognized the importance of these disclosures and brought them to the public's attention.

The more than 300 hours of televised hearings carried by the three commercial networks on a rotational basis cost them a combined total of $10 million in lost advertising revenue. (Interestingly, the Public Broadcasting Service attracted $1 million in donations through their coverage of these hearings.) That the public wanted these hearings televised was determined by the audience surveys. They showed that on an average day 30 percent of the viewing audience tuned in to the hearings (the others chose to watch the other networks' routine fare). When it was over, only 15 percent of the nation had failed to see at least one session of the hearings.

It is significant that all of the aforementioned examples of government misconduct, and not just the Watergate affair, were eventually brought into the open and disseminated by the mass media. This is no accident. Nor is it based on a unique American cultural trait favoring truthfulness. But it does reflect the economic fact that unlike any other major communications system, including the British and French, the American government does not have a part in the financial support of the mass media, nor in the selection of the persons who are involved in its operation. The much-maligned advertising dollar has, as we shall see, protected the mass media from government control as much as has the First Amendment. But this leaves one very important area unprotected.

Who's Watching the Media

While the federal government has an interlocking arrangement of checks and balances designed to avert consolidation of power, the press, protected by the First Amendment and functioning as another control over the government, is itself responsible to no one. And this is where the media does possess power, the power inherent in control over information. With the exception of the limitations imposed by the libel laws, the media can, through carelessness or design, distort the news and mislead the public. And to the extent that public attitudes feed back into the political and policy equation, the absence of a check or balance against the media represents a potential threat to the body politic.

Evidence of serious defects in the information provided the public is quite common. The Op Ed pages of most newspapers rarely print articles opposed to the newspaper's editorial position. In television the problem is more serious, because most people feel that filmed reports don't lie. But of course they do. Government action against public disturbances always shows the poor and misbegotten being trounced by police or the military. Cameramen are safe behind government lines. Sympathy invariably goes out to the crowd despite the fact that it is disturbing the peace, might have unreasonable demands, or might not even represent the wishes of the majority.

There is an even more serious problem posed by an unchecked and unbridled press, and that is that it will begin to think that it knows what is best for others, that it will sit in judgment on the issues that are in contention. The information that flows from this tainted source is propaganda, not news. There is ample evidence today that many journalists see themselves as latter-day churchmen in possession of a more sensitive moral conscience than the rest of their countrymen. They are becoming a lesser clergy, seeking to guide the public rather than being content to inform it. In a democracy a poorly informed public is the greatest threat to its own well-being.

To avoid issues that are loaded with emotional commitments—such as South Africa, Israel, Ireland, abortion, and sexual perversion—while illustrating faulty news coverage, we turn to the oil crises of 1973–74 and 1978–79. These were the most important nonmilitary events since the Great Depression of the 1930s. For most Americans, the first crisis seemed to leap full-grown from nowhere on October 17, 1973, when the Arabs announced an embargo on petroleum shipments to the United States supposedly to extort Western support in the Arab–Israeli conflict. By the time the embargo was lifted, on March 19, 1974, the price of oil had quadrupled.

The second crisis resulted from the Iranian Revolution. Iran, the fourth largest oil producer, ceased production on December 26, 1978. The Arabs hitched a ride on the growing shortage by cutting back their own production, thereby forcing the price of petroleum to rise worldwide. Overall, oil prices jumped eighteen-fold, from $2 a barrel to $35 a barrel in six years, creating a massive inflation.

How well did the media cover these events? How did they explain the causes, effects, and alternative solutions to these major crises? Was the public properly informed? These were news events not as loaded with moral judgment as so many we face in today's world. They called for straightforward research, with information garnered from all sides of the issue. But they were not handled in this manner by the television networks.

The Media Institute in Washington, D.C., made a detailed study of over 1,400 oil-crisis reports during this period. It concluded that the television networks failed to give the public sufficient information to make an informed judgment.

Over 75 percent of the information reported was supplied by the government. Outside experts were used as a source of information in only 2 percent of the reports, and industry in only 9 percent. The television networks identified past government policy as a possible cause of the crisis in only 18 percent of the reports. It put the principal blame on the oil industry and OPEC in 72 percent of the reports.

The media depicted price as the problem rather than as a possible solution. There would have been no shortage and no gas lines had the price of oil been permitted to reflect relative scarcity as it evolved. Rising prices would have "rationed" supply among the most urgent or valuable uses. Keeping prices artificially low brought out marginal users to create the long lines and the scarcity that developed. Yet the use of price as a form of control was discussed in only 15 percent of the reports. Half the reports called for rationing or mandatory conservation. Typical government solutions.

The media accepted OPEC claims that the embargo was a political rather than an economic weapon, yet the fact that oil was "slipping through the embargo" for those willing to pay higher prices made its economic character quite clear.

The television viewer was told in only 8 percent of the reports that increased domestic production could eliminate our dependence on foreign oil. Government policies had until then discouraged exploration. One month after the embargo, Congress passed the Alaska Pipeline Bill. It was too late for the short term but it helped in the long run.

A typical befogging report on the evening news would read: "All across the country, oil is not only expensive but it is in short supply" (ABC, February 28, 1979). The issue was presented as two problems rather than as a problem and its solution. The journalists had not done their homework. The government was always featured as the source of the solution, rarely as the cause of the problem. In the oil crisis there was little about which to be indignant, as in reporting on South Africa, so the poor quality of the work showed through. Moral posturing could not fill in for research, as it does in so many other issues.

The power of television lies not in its intrinsic ability to direct the viewers but in the reporters' use of this facility to inform or misinform them. There is only one real solution to this problem and it will probably have to be written into law: All sides of every issue must be presented, and this includes filmed reporting. Unfortunately, public policy in this regard has recently adopted the very opposite tact: The "fairness doctrine" which was only halfheartedly enforced over the years, instead of being given teeth, was rescinded by the Federal Communications Commission in 1987.

The Fairness Doctrine

The fairness doctrine was often confused with the so-called "equal time" law, which requires that all political candidates have equal access to the electronic media. The fairness doctrine was quite different. It dealt with *issues*, not with people. The doctrine did not require equal time for opposing views but simply called for some expression of the other side of the issue. It need not have been in the same broadcast or even by a representative of the opposing view. It simply required that sometime, somewhere in the station's programming the opposing opinion would find expression. It was a very weak assurance of fairness.

The problem was that there had never been a similar requirement regarding the printed media. The logic of applying this doctrine solely to the electronic media had been that there were, at the time, too few television stations for both sides of an issue to be assured access to the public and, therefore, each station owner had been asked to provide a rounded perspective of political and social issues. Today the media environment is not what it was 40 years ago. Today the public has at its disposal more television signals than newspapers. Asymmetry in the treatment of the two principal media became apparent. There was no longer justification for treating print and electronic media differently. However, instead of Congress's assuming the responsibility by *strengthening* the fairness doctrine and applying it to all media, it was perceived as a restriction of free speech of those who own and those who operate the media, and was dropped entirely.

When, in August 1987, the FCC abandoned the fairness doctrine, the then-chairman, Dennis Patrick, wrote in the official statement:

> the First Amendment does not guarantee a fair press, only a free press. . . . Faith in democracy entails a belief that political wisdom and virtue will sustain themselves in the free market of ideas without government intervention. As Jefferson put it, "It is error that needs the support of government. Truth can stand alone." . . . There are risks, but we as a people have elected to bear the risks of freedom rather than the greater risks which attend government control of the press.[5]

This almost poetic statement of the principal of freedom and the danger of governmental intervention is unassailable except for glaring inconsistencies and contradictions in public policy. Whose freedom of speech is guaranteed by the Constitution, that of the owners and operators of the mass media or that of the general public? The law now allows the broadcast of racial, religious, and sexual insults over the mass media under the guise of free speech, and it allows the mass media to broadcast only one side of an issue. The assurance that "the truth will out," that the public will know right from wrong without a comprehensive picture of the issue, is difficult to accept.

The law prohibits the advertising of cigarettes on any medium of electronic communication under FCC jurisdiction. This is not perceived as a violation of free speech. Why is one's physical well-being a greater concern than one's intellectual and moral well-being? More people have died from bad ideas than from bad products. In this century alone, the two world wars and the communist revolution have brought more death and crippled more people than any product, indeed than any disease.

In another inconsistency, the FCC regulations allow noncommercial (public) television to broadcast paid-for advertising of nonprofit organizations but not of commercial organizations. They may also editorialize on issues, but they may not support or oppose candidates for public office. This too is a strange definition of free speech and the First Amendment privilege.

What constitutes free speech and what constitutes the public interest is treated in a most sloppy fashion. Indeed, it appears that fashion rather than logic plays the greater role in defining the First Amendment.

The fairness doctrine addressed a problem that has now become a serious threat to the public interest. In its absence we have placed complete reliance on the fairness of the journalistic fraternity and the owners of the media. They are our source of information, ideas, and entertainment. We must hope that what they provide is untainted by their personal views. But hope is a weak reed. The old saw that total power corrupts totally applies here. We have already touched upon this problem in this chapter and will look into it further in Chapter 7.

The fact is, we interfere in industrial and commercial activity through the antitrust laws. These laws serve as the "rules of the game." The legal and medical professions also have their rules written into law. Why is journalism and entertainment so much more sacred that it is unbound by even the most minimal legal requirements? Would freedom of speech and the First Amendment be in jeopardy if there were rules that required that both sides of an issue be presented at all times? Would this not be truer to the intent of the First Amendment? Current policy confines the privilege of free speech to those who own the facilities of mass communications and those who are employed in it. They have not proven to be disinterested parties. To expect them to be is unnatural.

Decency

Coca-Cola, Campbell Soup Co., Ralston Purina Co., Kimberly Clark Corp., and others were upset. They felt that many of the programs that carried their advertisements were unacceptable ad vehicles. And now they were faced with a letter-writing campaign

and threat of boycott as a result of a one-woman crusade. Terry
Rakolta, a 41-year-old housewife and mother, took steps against
the indecency that appears increasingly to have made itself a part
of television programming.

How did the networks come to this? Few will deny that
television at the end of the eighties was not the same television we
saw in the sixties. It can be argued that new technology (about
which we will have more to say later) has so cut into network
audiences that they have been forced to lower their standards in
order to hold on to viewers. But this is only part of the answer.
How is it that the public accepts the trash it is shown? And it is
not only the subject matter that is in question, it is the attitude
toward the subject that has changed.

In one program a man makes sexual advances to his mature
stepmother and it is presented in lighthearted fashion. Another
program shines a positive light on sexual perversion, and incest
is now just another family affair. Lewdness is commonplace and
all bodily functions are on the screen, not just sexual intercourse
but defecation and urination as well. Violence can't be disgusting
enough. In 1989 the president of NBC, Robert Wright, told the
Association of National Advertisers, "We are no longer in the
position of being able to have arbitrary standards that may or may
not reflect viewership standards." And the networks had always
been thought of as the last bastion of family entertainment.

The sad part of it is that the community's standards have
declined. In the competitive quest for ratings and profits, the
media follow—they don't lead—the audience. People today
permit into their homes programs they would never have allowed
their children or even themselves to watch only a few years
ago. Evidently, parents either don't watch television with their
children, or they have abandoned all standards and feel no
embarrassment.

Years ago, when *Life* magazine went under, it might have tried
to survive with pornography. Not just the law, but society, would
have rejected it. The company knew this. The damage to the

company's image, even for the sake of survival, was not, in those days, worth the price.

Nevertheless, the president of NBC and his colleagues at the other networks, and the broadcasters who allow trash programs to go out over the airwaves, have all opted out of responsibility. The responsibility rests with that vague body called the community, often referred to as "society." Drug addicts, perverts, juvenile delinquents, and adult criminals are all free of responsibility. They are "victims of society." Now it is the networks' turn to claim to be a victim. The fact is, the individual has responsibility for his actions whether he was brought up in a slum or is the president of a television network.

A great deal of the responsibility also rests with the law. Most people respect the law. However, if the law gives them license to do today what it disallowed yesterday, they will ask no questions. They are quick to adapt themselves to the new reality. And the media follow quickly on the heels of what is permitted. They are a reflection of society.

The Chairman of the Federal Communications Commission decided to take on the issue of decency in the media. He banned "indecency"—defined as the showing of body parts on television. So strange are today's standards that the attempt to impose some standard of decency in broadcasting is opposed by an advocacy group called Action For Children's Television. Clearly there is a need for a standard that can be enforced, preferably by the industry, so that the lowest tastes don't determine the character of American culture.

Both in the quality of its news reporting and in the quality of the public entertainment it is offering, America's mass communications system requires more self-discipline.

2 The System

Is Television Replacing the Other Media?

One of the reasons for the general impression that television has awesome power is the disappearance of many of the giants in the newspaper field during television's development as the nationwide medium.

In 1963, the nation's second largest newspaper, the *New York Daily Mirror*, went under. This was followed by the agonizing death of the venerable *New York Herald Tribune* in 1966, and some months later by the demise of the *New York World-Telegram and Sun* and *New York Journal American*—all of which had a long and respected history in American journalism. Nor is this problem confined to New York City. The *Boston Herald Traveler* folded, as did the *Newark News* in New Jersey and the *Daily News* in Washington, D.C. Indeed, nationwide, in the years 1950–67, when television had its most rapid growth, 330 newspapers, or about 1 out of 5, suspended operation.[1] Today only 43 cities in the United States are left with competing dailies.

It is easy to generalize from these observations that the newspaper industry is in trouble. Since these difficulties coincided with the growth of television, it is also tempting to conclude that newspapers were being replaced by the newer technology. Indeed, it is often said that newspapers are becoming an obsolete form of mass communication. The weight of the evidence, however, clearly shows that such conclusions are unfounded.

Available data indicate that newspaper readership in general has increased. Thus, although the number of dailies has declined from about 2,000 in 1920 to 1,800 in 1988, their circulation has increased from 28 million per day in 1920 to about 63 million per day in 1988. In effect, in a period when the national population more than doubled, and radio and television were introduced, newspaper circulation increased by about 125 percent. Newspaper revenues from advertising increased even more rapidly than circulation during the 1920–88 period, rising from about $300 million in 1920 to nearly $31 *billion* in 1988.

When compared, in absolute terms, the importance of the printed medium looms even larger than television. Therefore, the economic fuel that operates America's mass communications system is the advertising expenditures of American business. Over $118 billion was spent on all forms of advertising in the United States in 1988. Of this sum, what is conventionally

Table 1   Where Advertising Money Goes by Type of Mass Media, 1988 (in billions of dollars)

Daily Newspapers	$ 31.1
Television	25.6
Radio	7.8
Magazines*	6.0
Total	$ 70.5

*Magazines earned another $6 billion from subscription fees.

Source: *Advertising Age*, May 15, 1989. Prepared by McCann-Erickson, Inc.

referred to as the mass media—newspapers, television, radio, and magazines—received about $70 billion or 60 percent, and of these $70 billion the daily newspaper is the recipient of more than $31 billion or 44 percent of the advertising money spent on all the mass media. In addition, newspapers receive over $5 billion a year from subscriptions and sales at newsstands. The newspaper industry's total revenue (exclusive of the wire services) thus approaches $36 billion a year. This is 38 percent more than the revenue received by the entire television broadcasting industry in 1989.

These facts may come as a surprise to the many people who have the mistaken impression that television is today the dominant medium in the United States. Television does command a lot of attention, but in many respects, particularly in economic terms, it is considerably behind newspapers.

How, then, do we explain the high rate of failure among newspapers?

Looking back at the 1950–67 period, we see that while 330 newspapers failed, 303 new dailies were started—an average of 17 new dailies a year. Of the 303 new ventures, 166 survived to become established enterprises. This is a success rate of 55 percent. Significantly, and in this lies the explanation, most of the successes were in cities with a population of under 500,000. The problem of survival is a problem facing newspapers in the big cities.

Why Newspapers Fail

What troubled the big-city newspaper? Excess printing capacity, rising labor costs (specifically, of typesetters), and the inability to adopt radically new technology were some of the problems. But these were not the critical factors. There was a more fundamental problem.

Since advertisers necessarily watch the circulation figures, the two, circulation and advertising, are closely related. Newspaper economists agree that if a big-city newspaper's circulation exceeds that of its principal competitor by a 2:1 margin, this will prove fatal to the relatively smaller newspaper, no matter how large it might be.

The extreme sensitivity of newspapers to declining circulation is due in large part to the structure of their advertising rates. These are based on a sliding scale whereby substantial advertisers obtain substantial discounts. Thus, a big advertiser can get as much as 35-percent discount by doubling the amount of space he buys in a single newspaper in a given year. To obtain this discount, the advertiser is encouraged to give all his business to a single newspaper in a given community. That newspaper is frequently the one that has the edge in circulation. So he is induced to take his advertising away from the relatively smaller newspaper and place it in the competing daily. It is the pursuit of the discount that whiplashes the runner-up even though it has a large circulation and tries to compete by lowering its own rates.

The *New York Daily Mirror*, which folded in 1963 when it was the second-largest morning newspaper in the United States, had a daily circulation of over 800,000 when it closed down. Nevertheless, it was substantially behind the competing morning tabloid, the *New York Daily News*, and so was the loser in the ensuing advertising war.

The *New York Herald Tribune* faced a similar problem. The *Tribune* died because in the years between 1955 and 1965, its advertising lineage had dropped below the break-even point, or by a total of 1,911,395 lines. This represented $2,675,000 a year in lost revenues, or $390,000 more than the annual wage bill for its 277 printers. The *Tribune* could not have survived even if its printers had decided to work for nothing. Therefore, even the use of the latest technology, which would have reduced its wage bill, would not have sufficed.[2]

What lies behind the sudden, desperate pressure for newspaper circulation in the nation's big cities?

The explanation is found in the decentralization of America's urban centers. As the wealthy and middle-class whites moved into the suburbs, the retail shopping center and department store branches followed them. And so did the newspaper circulation and advertising revenue that supported the old, well-established big-city dailies. In effect, social forces outside the industry reshaped its character in the second half of the twentieth century. The issue is thus not technological but sociological. Newspapers are not becoming technologically obsolete. Rather, their markets are changing location and they are in a state of transition.

Tripping Over the Wire Services

One of the impediments to establishing a new newspaper in a large city is the high cost of subscribing to the major wire services. Wire services are to the newspapers what television networks are to television broadcasting stations: They are their main source of information. (Television-network news departments also employ the wire services to supplement their own sources.) Privately owned, these wire services serve as the primary source of nearly all of the national and international news available to the American public.

Implicitly, when we speak of the wire services, we refer to the most prominent: Associated Press (AP), United Press International (UPI), and Reuters. *Editors & Publishers Yearbook*, however, lists over 300 domestic and foreign syndicates, ranging from the three largest to small, one-man operations. About 200 provide straight news and pictures. Dozens more specialize in subject matter ranging from editorial cartoons to household features, religious features, and subject matter of interest to very specialized groups. The latter include the Jewish Telegraphic Agency, the National Catholic News Service, Women's News Service, Science News Service, and the Auto News Syndicate. But the three major services are the ones that provide the worldwide, in-depth news coverage without which a major daily would be lost.

Given the scope of their operations, the big three are in fact stretched very thin. Reuters, which is British owned, employs 3,600 journalists and editors. Of the two major American news services, AP employs 2,000 and UPI 1,800. In addition to permanent staff, all the wire services employ "stringers," who provide information on a call basis.

Reuters' staff is the most extensively distributed worldwide. About 70 percent of its staff are abroad. At AP only 25 percent are abroad and at UPI 33 percent. The American organizations focus heavily on domestic news, which for the American media is of prime interest. Their revenues are similarly structured. Over 80 percent of Reuters' revenues are from foreign sources, whereas the two American news services earn less than 25 percent of their revenues abroad.

Though the three major news services are all privately owned, they differ radically in structure. Reuters is a British firm specializing in foreign news. After going through hard times, it became the most financially successful of the three by establishing an information-retrieval service based on computers and focusing on financial and economic information. UPI is a private company established by the E. W. Scripps organization in 1907. The AP, on the other hand, is a news cooperative established in 1848. To supplement the work of its journalists, AP receives local news from its respective participating newspapers for distribution among its members.

All three agencies together have a gross revenue of less than $500 million and only Reuters can be said to profitable. AP, because of its cooperative structure, tends to break even as its members cover its losses. UPI, on the other hand, has been fighting for its life. Indeed, in 1983 the Scripps organization sold its struggling news service to unusual owners, the Media News Corporation, a company newly formed by the two owners of a Nashville-based cable television system. The second-biggest news agency in the United States was taken over by William Geissler and Douglas Ruhe, products of the counter-culture of the 1960s. Both served prison sentences, one for draft evasion and the other as a result of his participation in civil rights demonstrations. They are both members of the Baha'i faith.[3]

The principal cause for the slide that hit UPI followed on the decline of competing major dailies in America's major cities. Only 43 cities remain with two or more dailies. In the absence of a competitor, the single remaining newspaper doesn't have to subscribe to more than one news service. There is no longer the fear that the competing paper might receive a news advantage from the other news services—which is what had compelled every daily to subscribe to all the major services in the past. Today, in the absence of local competition, most newspaper publishers choose AP and drop the other services.

By 1985, UPI had declined to the point where it had to file for protection from its creditors under Chapter 11 of the U.S. bankruptcy code. UPI was then serving 800 newspapers and 3,300 broadcasters, while AP was serving 1,260 newspapers and 5,700 broadcasters.

Ironically, an important factor limiting the entry of new dailies in the major cities is the relatively high fee required by the major wire services. They require evidence of survivability in the form of substantial working capital. In addition, a subscriber has to put down a one-year advance and sign a five-year contract. The price of the service, however, is based *not* on subscriber circulation, which for a newcomer would be low, but on the size of the market in which he operates. In the large cities, this involves a very substantial annual cost for just one wire service. When combined with a one-year advance, this means that there is a very stiff entry fee, and double this sum for two major wire services. This cost could be a serious obstacle for a newcomer, certainly more serious than the presence of television, which, as we shall see later, is not a serious competitor for newspaper advertising revenue or its audience.

On the Down Staircase: The Radio Networks

The reputation of television as the "spoiler," representing a powerful competitive force on the media scene, is more deserved for its effect on the radio networks than for any imagined effect on newspapers. Its impact on the radio networks can be described in one word—devastating.

For the generation or two that grew up on *Captain Midnight, The Shadow, Fred Allen, Fibber McGee & Molly, The Great Gildersleeve,* and *Gabriel Heater*—and who are now the nation's decision makers, its congressmen, academicians, regulators, and writers—television left them only fond memories of the highly successful radio network news and entertainment medium. It is with some cause, therefore, that today's opinion makers and policy makers are in awe of the power of television and, inferentially, of all mass media. This experience makes them believe much of the mythology surrounding mass communications, especially television.

In 1950, before television's explosive growth, the four national radio networks were all doing well. ABC, CBS, NBC, and MBS (Mutual Broadcasting System) together had a nationwide audience and earned profits of $19 million, before taxes, on revenues of $106 million. That same year the four struggling television networks (Dumont, now defunct, was the fourth) lost $10 million on revenues of $55 million.[4]

Since then, television has drastically changed the radio business, forcing it to become a local medium. The radio network entertainment shows are all gone, replaced by television. This has given rise to the widespread belief that radio is in a state of depression, if not on its way out as a mass medium.

The decline of the radio networks, however, should not be confused with the state of well-being of radio broadcasting. By shifting the focus of its attention from a nationwide audience to the local audience, radio broadcasting underwent an unprecedented boom at the very time that radio networking was slipping into oblivion.

In 1950, when television was still in its infancy, there were 2,100 radio stations in the United States. Thirty-eight years later, in 1988 there were 10,600 radio stations on-the-air, five times the number before television. The revenues of radio broadcasting stations rocketed in this period, from \$334 million in 1950 to \$7.8 billion in 1988.[5] Radio networks had declined in importance as a source of programming, but radio itself prospered as a mass medium.

A number of factors shaped this transformation. These include the explosive growth of the radio audience as a result of low-cost transistor radios. The number of radios in the United States increased from 85 million in 1950 to over 400 million in 1988. As a result of the rise in number of suburban commuters, automobile radios alone increased from 18 million in use in 1950, to 100 million in 1988. On the other side of the coin, the low cost of entry into radio broadcasting attracted local investors, who saw radio as a prestigious small business. Thus, while individual communications companies, particularly the giants, were going under, radio broadcasting was expanding.

Creative Destruction

The giants among newspapers, magazines, and radio experienced in the 1960s what is referred to by economists as the process of "creative destruction." Suburbanization and the advent of television shook the established corporations to their foundations. Firms that seemed to be the eternal powers with a dominant, deeply entrenched position in mass communications, at one moment, were transformed in the next moment into small businesses (for example, the radio networks)—if they survived at all. As a form of mass communication, however, newspapers, magazines, and radio were not rendered obsolete; they boomed. Their internal structures were altered and their giants were humbled but, as industries, they thrived. In a creative, free, and open economic environment, power is transitory, almost fleeting, indeed perhaps nonexistent. Who would believe, for example, that *Life* magazine would ever cease publication? The process of creative destruction had removed from the scene a publication that only three short years before had sufficient influence to bring about the resignation of a Supreme Court justice. Like the radio and the newspaper, the magazine was also in the process of change.

The 9,600 weekly, monthly, and quarterly magazines and journals published in the United States range in character from the most widely read (*Reader's Digest, TV Guide, and Modern Maturity* each with about 17 million circulation) to thousands of small and obscure publications that cater to specific needs of different groups of readers. The evidence indicates, however, that the future of the magazine business belongs to the small specialized publications.

To survive today a magazine has to satisfy a special interest. Zoology, occultism, antiques, high fidelity, dress-making, dogs, bowling, poetry, travel, indeed in almost any subject, one inevitably has several publications from which to choose. Similarly, each religious, social, trade, professional and technical group is served by a number of periodicals fighting for a greater share of that market.

The financial support for these publications is based on their specialized readership and the advertiser's interest in reaching just those particular readers. The audience of these publications is defined by the publication's subject matter. Thus, magazines have become the vehicle for advertising special products for special audiences. Advertisers of widely consumed products, on the other hand, look to television to reach the mass audience. The victim of these developments has been the mass-circulation magazine, which has all but disappeared. Thus, such former giants of the communications industry as *Collier's, Saturday Evening Post, Look*, and *Life* have passed into publishing history.

Initially, the mass-circulation magazines tried to compete with television. In the early 1960s, *Life* and *Look* fought a circulation battle to see which (like television) could reach the greatest number of subscribers. Indeed, *Life* bought 1.5 million subscribers from the defunct *Saturday Evening Post* in order to reach what proved to be its peak circulation of 8.5 million in 1968. But this larger circulation required higher advertising rates. In 1968, *Life* had to charge $64,000 for a color page—much more than the cost of a minute of prime time on television.

Madison Avenue wouldn't buy. There was a 13-percent decline in advertising pages that year and the price had to be cut to $54,000 a color page. But, for the advertisers, the cost of reaching a thousand homes was still too high, about $7.71 compared to $3.60 for television. An important distinction between magazines and television that explains some of this price disparity is the concept of *circulation*. Circulation is the number of buyers or subscribers of the publication. The *readership*, particularly of the general magazine, is at least five times that number. In addition, the magazine, or any printed medium, can be used for recall by the subscriber. Television, on the other hand, reaches its audience but once with each message. The advantage of television, on the other hand, is that it employs both sight and sound. It also reaches the disinterested viewer, who does not flip channels as readily as he flips pages in a magazine in order to avoid a message that doesn't interest him. The latter makes readership an unreliable index of an ad's audience. In other words, the television audience is more of a captive than is the self-programmed reader of periodicals.

In the final analysis, advertisers preferred television to magazines as the vehicle for mass-marketing. Their decision was also based, in part, on an awareness that the circulation of the major magazines was being subsidized. It didn't reflect a real demand on the part of the public. This is evident from a comparison between the price the public is willing to pay for more specialized magazines and what it is prepared to pay for general (mass) magazines.

Between 1947 and 1970, *Life* magazine's *newsstand* sales fell from 2.5 million to 210,000, even though it had a relatively low newsstand price of 50 cents. Relatively more specialized magazines, such as *Playboy* (at the time, $1 a copy) and *Cosmopolitan* (then, $1 a copy), on the other hand, were able to obtain 80 percent and 88 percent of their circulation, respectively, from newsstand sales despite higher prices. The truly mass-circulation magazines, with their generalized content, could only maintain their huge circulations by practically giving away their publication to subscribers for about 12 cents a copy, although at the time it cost the publisher over 40 cents to produce and distribute. The public, it appears, found the content of such magazines of insufficient continuing interest to warrant paying a higher price. This attitude was not lost on the advertisers.[6]

Stopgap measures had been employed in the fight for survival. Several magazines cut their physical size. A mere three-sixteenths-of-an-inch trim in page size reportedly saved *Life* $500,000 a year, although most reductions in page size have been substantially greater (*McCall's, Ladies' Home Journal, Esquire, Fortune*). But for *Life* magazine such savings merely postponed the inevitable. The only long-term solution for periodicals is to stake out a subgroup in the mass audience that will permit a sharp cutback in costly circulation with a less than proportionate reduction in advertising rates.

This was the path taken by Time, Inc., following the collapse of *Life*. They first marketed *Money*, a consumer's magazine aimed at the middle-income shopper. This was followed, about a year later (1974), with *People*, a biography-gossip-news magazine. To avoid the pitfalls introduced by sharply rising postal rates, *People* is not sold by subscription but over the counter in supermarkets and drugstores. The new publication had a full-time staff of only 34. Its initial price was only 35 cents and its first press run was a relatively modest 1.4 million copies—compared with *Life's* peak printing of 8.5 million. These more modest proportions permitted Time, Inc., to lower its advertising rate to one half that required by *Life* in its heyday.

To Specialize or Not to Specialize

The demise of *Look* and *Life* frightened other mass-circulation magazines. These include magazines that specialize in very large subgroups, such as men or women. One such publication sought unsuccessfully to anticipate and to fend off the fate of the more general mass-circulation magazines.

In an analysis of magazine economics that appeared in the *Columbia Journalism Review*, Chris Welles compared the attempts of *McCall's* and the *Ladies' Home Journal* to face up to these problems.[7] He noted that the major magazines catering to the women's market have a dual personality. They are mass-circulation publications that serve a special audience. Thus *McCall's*, which had a 1970 circulation of over 8 million and *Ladies' Home Journal*, which had a circulation of nearly 7 million, specialize in the homemaker market. By comparison, men's magazines tend to serve smaller audiences. Thus, *Playboy*, the largest "man's" magazine, has half the circulation reported by the largest "woman's" magazine. Women's interests are much more homogeneous—which contributes to the large size of their audience.

Despite the mass-circulation character of the leading women's magazines, they have substantial advertiser support because they are aimed at the homemaker, who buys most of the food, drugs, toiletries, and related goods that are subject to mass-marketing. Nevertheless, fearing the fate of the general mass-circulation magazines, *McCall's*, in spite of being a reputedly profitable operation, made a major attempt to break away from the homemaker format. In 1969, it brought in Shana Alexander, a *Life* columnist, to serve as editor in a premature attempt to reach a sophisticated "concerned" subgroup of the mass women's market. She shifted the focus of *McCall's* away from the home to world issues. The result: Advertisers, fearing a loss of the homemaker atmosphere that the old format had provided for their products, began to withdraw their support, while the *Ladies' Home Journal*, which retained its homemaker format, saw its revenues increase by 19 percent in 1969–70.

McCall's eventually brought in a new editor who tried, unsuccessfully, to recapture the old *McCall's* clientele. In 1973, its owner, the Norton Simon Corporation, sold *McCall's* to a more optimistic investor, the owners of the Hyatt Hotels. The *McCall's* experiment, although unsuccessful, was farsighted.

The cost of operating mass-circulation magazines is prohibitive today. As Welles pointed out in his article, the cost of postage, paper, and printing will continue to rise. But major increases in advertising rates are difficult to administer, since mass-circulation magazines are already more expensive than television, the principal vehicle for access to large audiences. Therefore, the only alternative is to increase subscription rates. This, however, will cut down on the circulation of supposedly mass-circulation magazines. Today subscription revenue accounts for half their income.

It is not easy to back down: The transition is costly. Significantly, the audience that *McCall's* tried to reach was eventually tackled with some success, but on a much smaller scale, by entirely new publications such as *Ms.*, which focuses on the feminist market.

The process of creative destruction observed at work in network radio is thus also at work in the magazine field. Such reputedly powerful organizations as Time, Inc., Curtis Publishing Co., and Crowell Collier simply could not influence the public or the advertisers to continue to support their publications. This is a strange situation for enterprises supposedly in the busi-

Table 2   Ten Leading Magazines, 1988

	CIRCULATION (MILLIONS)
TV Guide	16.9
Modern Maturity	16.7
Reader's Digest	16.5
National Geographic	10.5
Better Homes & Gardens	8.0
Woman's Day	6.0
Family Circle	5.7
McCall's	5.3
Good Housekeeping	5.2
Ladies' Home Journal	5.1

Source: Audit Bureau of Circulation.

ness of influencing. It stands in stark contrast to the mythology that attributes to these "media baronies" the awesome ability to seize their audiences by their collective psyches and shape their attitudes on almost anything of importance.

Table 2 lists the ten leading magazines and their circulation. It should be noted, however, that their readership exceeds their circulation by three or four times, which explains why they are still attractive to national advertisers.

On the Fringe

Several substantial, though relatively minor, media operate on the fringe of mass communications. They are not significant in terms of advertising but are very important in noncommercial matters. One such medium is the weekly newspaper. These publications serve a specifically defined geographic area with neighborhood news. The local merchants, artisans, and families use its columns and classified sections to communicate with one another.

In 1989 there were 7,800 weeklies published in the United States, with a combined circulation exceeding 28 million. The weeklies claim a readership of 111 million or about 4 readers per copy.

A central advertising agency—American Newspaper Representatives Incorporated—serves most of the weeklies as a clearinghouse for national advertising. The suburban market that many weeklies serve has grown substantially in wealth as well as in size in recent years. These developments have not gone unnoticed by the major communications companies. Thus, Time, Inc., purchased over 25 weekly newspapers in the Chicago area.

There are also media that cater to large special groups. Most of these fall into one of three categories: black, religious, or foreign language. There are currently 163 black-oriented publications in the United States with a total circulation of 5.1 million or nearly one copy for each black family in America. In addition, there are about 385 radio stations with some black programming, including 188 devoted entirely to black programming. At least one such station is located in every major city in the United States, and in many smaller southern cities.[8]

The foreign-language media also operate on the fringe of the major media. Once an extremely important source of information and entertainment for millions of foreign-born Americans, their popularity has declined with the decline in immigration. Nevertheless, there are still hundreds of general-interest periodicals published in 34 different languages, with a combined circulation exceeding 2 million. The largest circulation is credited to 54 Spanish-language newspapers, which have a combined circulation of about 1.5 million. They serve the fastest-growing foreign-language audience in the United States. In addition, 285 radio stations in the United States broadcast some foreign-language programs; of these, 237 broadcast in Spanish.

But the largest group of mass media focusing on a special audience in the United States are the religiously oriented newspapers and periodicals. While many of them have very small circulations,

16 major religious periodicals have, each, circulations exceeding 500,000. Religious publications have a combined circulation of more than 35 million—or nearly one copy for every two households in the nation.[9] One such publisher, the Worldwide Church of God, which has only 85, 000 churchgoers, distributes 8 million copies of *Plain Truth* each month. The sect receives over $50 million a year from members and sympathizers.[10] In addition, in 1989, *Editor & Publishers Yearbook* listed 172 religiously oriented newspapers.

Since, in general, religious publications are financed through dues and donations paid to the main religious organizations, commercial advertising plays a relatively unimportant role in their support. In addition to the print media, there are 930 radio stations devoted to religious programming.[11]

The media based on geographical identity (weeklies), race, religion, and ethnic backgrounds offer the mass media serious competition in the realm of ideas. Their impact is small in economic terms, but, contrary to the accepted mythology they are important opinion makers.

The Age of Television

Without eliminating any of the existing forms of mass communications, television established itself as the sole *national* medium. At the fulcrum of today's television system in the United States are the networks, with which three out of every four television stations are affiliated. The local broadcast stations provide these stations provide the networks with regular, assured access to their local television audiences. In exchange, the networks provide these stations with programs through much of the day. Not only are these programs provided free, but the stations are paid a percentage of the advertising revenue that the networks receive from national advertisers.

Stations that by virtue of their geographical location reach large audiences cost the advertisers a higher price for their inclusion in the network lineup than stations located in smaller markets. Each network affiliate receives a portion of its price. Overall, network affiliates receive about 12 percent of the advertising money received by the networks (and free programming). These funds account for approximately 11 percent of the total revenue received by television broadcasting stations.[12] The rest of the broadcasters' income is obtained from local advertisers and from the national "spot" market, discussed below.

The size of the audience "delivered" to the advertiser by the network is a function of the number of cities in the network lineup, the time of day the commercial is shown, and the popularity of the program in which the advertisement was included. These three factors determine the price paid by the advertiser.

The broadcasters have practically no say over any of these factors. They cannot affect the number of persons choosing to live in their market area, nor the caliber or popularity of the network's choice of programs. Their facilities are in a very real sense conduits for the national television networks. Programming decisions are made by the local broadcasters for the weekends. These generally account for about half of their broadcasting hours. But the networks supply the programs for the prime hours when the audiences are largest.

For those hours for which the networks do not provide programs the broadcasters buy programs from independent producers and from the "syndication market," which offers a large number of programs that have already been seen on television (reruns). The revenue obtained by broadcasters during those hours when they program for themselves is derived from local advertisers (used-car dealers, department stores, etc.) and the "spot market," consisting of regional and national advertisers who wish to advertise in selected markets rather than across-the-board in a network lineup. This "spot" money is channeled to broadcasters (by the advertising agencies) through station representatives who

Table 3   Sources of Television Revenue*

SOURCE	PERCENTAGE OF TOTAL
Network	46%
Spot	32%
Local	22%
Total	100%

*Including the three networks.
Source: FCC Release 05963, Table 1.

are, in effect, time brokers for the local stations. Most of these brokers or representatives are located in New York City. Some 60 such brokers represent nearly all the television and radio stations in the United States.

Local advertisers have accounted for about 39 percent of the average broadcaster's revenue and the regional and national "spot" market for about 50 percent of his revenue. The balance (11 percent), as already noted, is received from the networks.

Looking at the television industry as a whole, including the three television networks, we find a different composition for advertising revenue due to the substantial sum retained by the networks, as shown in Table 3.

Network Profitability

How rich are the television networks (not including their broadcasting stations)? When *combined*, the three networks grossed $7.6 billion in 1988. This would rank them as fifty-sixth in sales among *Fortune* magazine's list of the 500 largest industrial corporations. (Taken separately, of course, each network would rank lower.) Not only are 56 industrial companies larger than the three television networks *combined*, but so are many retailers and transportation companies.[13]

In 1988 the combined profit derived from the programming activities of the three television networks totaled $500 million. That comes to a 6.6-percent return on revenues, before taxes. This return on sales is slightly below the average for American industry as a whole. Hidden in this rather dull and uninspiring income picture, however, are the returns earned by the networks on their own broadcasting stations.

The television broadcasting networks each own a broadcasting station in each of America's largest cities. These are the industry's premier money-earners. In 1988, as a group, the network-owned stations had a combined gross revenue of $1.7 billion and reported operating profits of $826 million. By comparison as already noted above, that year the networks earned profits of only $500 million on gross revenues of $7.6 billion received from program production and network advertising. (These figures do not include the new Fox Network established by Ruppert Murdoch.)

The networks' television stations are clearly money-making machines. The network-owned stations as a group earned 47.4 percent on revenues while the networking part of their business had a profit margin of only 6.6 percent. As a result of the extraordinary profitability, the television industry as a whole

Table 4 Network Revenues and Profits, 1988
              (in millions of dollars)

| NETWORK | NO. STA'S | OWNED STATIONS | | NETWORKING | |
		REV.	PROFIT	REV.	PROFIT
ABC	8	$ 770	$417	$2,382	$178
CBS	5	382	152	2,185	42
NBC	7	590	257	3,018	280
FOX	[7]	[na]	[na]	[na]	[na]
Total	20	$1,742	$826	$7,585	$500

Source: *Broadcasting*, May 1, 1989, p. 35.

has an undeserved reputation for being enormously profitable. The fact is, the entire television broadcasting industry—with all broadcasting stations combined—is not as profitable as anyone of a dozen industrial corporations.

Because of their financial importance to the networks, the network-owned stations have been the Achilles heel of the television industry.   Broadcasting stations are licensed and regulated by the Federal Communications Commission. As a result, it is the lever upon which the federal government has kept a firm grip and, as we shall see in the following discussion, has tried to use it to influence the character of programming.

3 Media Ownership[1]

How Many Can Play?

In the United States, unlike any other country in the world, the publication of newspapers, magazines, and books involves virtually no regulation or licensing, something that is not true even for the local drugstore, building contractor, or restaurant. The commercial broadcasting stations, on the other hand, though entirely privately owned, are licensed by the federal government. The principal mechanism by which the government can exercise some authority over radio and television broadcasting is through the issuance and threatened withdrawal of these broadcasting licenses.

While all of the worthwhile broadcast licenses have long since been assigned, looking back we can agree with the many critics who point out that the degree of differentiation among competing applicants was generally illusory and that the assignment of a broadcaster's license was more often than not a reward for the group or company represented by the more clever or better-connected attorney.

44

Many of these critics would have preferred to see these licenses auctioned off to the highest bidder instead of being awarded free to the winning applicant. But delivering these licenses into the hands of the wealthiest contestants would hardly have been an improvement over the admittedly deficient system that was used.

In fact, some form of auction was involved. After exhaustive and expensive comparative hearings, nearly half of those who originally received a permit from the FCC to build a television station (preliminary to licensing) eventually sold their permit to the highest bidder. The profits, however, benefited the seller, not the public purse. A better approach would have been to conduct a lottery among the qualified contenders. The result would have been a considerable savings in legal fees and government expense. The winner of the lottery might then have been required to pay a fee representing the license's economic potential so that the public purse would have capitalized on some of the license's value, instead of allowing the first licensee all of the benefit from the capital gain. But that, of course, is all a part of history.

Whatever the original flaws in the government's method of assigning broadcast licenses, most of the really valuable licenses have long since gravitated into the hands of large broadcast companies referred to as "group owners."

By law, however, no group owner can own more than a dozen television stations, or more than one in the same market (city). For reasons we shall take up in some detail in Chapter 6, the government designed the television communications system so that it consists of hundreds of broadcasting stations each covering a relatively small geographic area, rather than regional coverage with each region being served by several stations.

In part, the highly fractionalized ownership of America's broadcast communications reflects a deeply rooted national distrust of powerful social, political, and economic institutions. Under America's unique banking system, for example, there are over 14,000 banks as contrasted to fewer than eight in most other countries. And none of the nation's more than 14,000 banks

may have a branch outside of its home state—a rule intended
to prevent the development of a nationwide money monopoly.
Even the powers of the central banks, the Federal Reserve
System, and the Federal Home Loan Bank are divided among a
dozen or more regional and district banks. Similarly, America's
educational system is based on over 15,000 local school districts,
and here the state governments have only limited authority and
the federal government has virtually no authority at all. Small
wonder that ownership should be such an important concern in
the operation of America's mass communications. But as we shall
see later, the application of this policy to television was a major
error.

The communications system is further divided between the
owners of the facilities (newspapers, radio, cable systems, and
television broadcasting stations) and the producers of the content
transmitted by these facilities. The producers of most of the
content are the major wire services, the television networks
and the more recently formed satellite transmissions of cable-
system producers. This distinction between the ownership of
the distribution facilities and the production of the content is
not clear-cut. Newspapers and radio and television stations also
produce some of their own material, while some wire services are
owned by important newspapers, and the networks own lucrative
radio and television broadcasting stations. Still, the distinction
is important in identifying the centers of decision-making within
the industry.

The owners of communications facilities—newspapers, cable
systems, and broadcasting stations—theoretically have the power
(and responsibility) to decide what their local audience will
see, hear, and read. In practical terms, however, television
broadcasters have, as we have already noted, almost no say in
the content of network programs or in their selection. And for
most station owners, production costs are too high to permit them
to produce effective programming on their own. In addition,
the flow of news into newspapers and radio stations today is

so voluminous that there is barely time to read through what is available for use each day, much less to check its veracity. For all practical purposes, the owners of the mass media are as dependent on their program and information suppliers for the content they transmit to the public as a retail merchant is dependent on his wholesaler for the merchandise he sells.

Thus, despite the atomized ownership structure of the communications facilities, most of the news and entertainment received by the American public are produced by five corporations: UPI, AP, CBS, ABC, and NBC. *Yet none of these enterprises is licensed or regulated in its production activities by any government agency—federal, state, or local.*

Only by threatening the networks' ownership of their lucrative broadcasting stations, which *are* licensed, or by regulations affecting the broadcasters' relationship with the networks, can the regulatory authority (FCC) influence the program decisions of the radio and television networks. Since newspapers are not licensed by any authority, the wire services are protected even from this indirect control.

As a result of the FCC's arm's-length relationship with the networks, there used to be an intense preoccupation with broadcasting stations. By changing the rules governing broadcasting, the FCC hoped to effect changes in programming. Since the Reagan Administration's anti-regulatory policy and the Supreme Court's decisions opposed to censorship, there has been a sharp decline in FCC involvement.

Rules of the Game

Once the Federal Communications Commission grants a license to operate a broadcasting station, it retains the authority to review the assignment every five years (radio licenses are granted for seven years). At that time the license can be renewed (which most are), revoked (very rare), or reissued with conditions. It is at this juncture that the FCC, if it had a desire to do so, could influence the station owner's policies regarding the station's programming. It could decide that there are too many commercials, or that the programming doesn't answer the local market's needs.

In addition to this discretionary interference, there are several basic rules that apply to all station owners. Until August 1987 the FCC maintained what was called the "fairness doctrine." This important rule required broadcasters to present all sides of an issue. This is now no longer the case. Of all the regulations the FCC has ever had, this was one of the most important. As we will discuss later, its cancellation has resulted in the appearance of bias even in news reporting, where the doctrine did not apply but which has been affected by its spirit. Special reports and political analyses are also changing as a result of this freedom to abandon objectivity. The anti-trust laws and the libel laws do not fill the need left by the absence of the "fairness doctrine."

To encourage a greater diversity in programming, the FCC, in 1971, passed a ruling that limited the network's access to prime time. The FCC forced open the otherwise monopolized prime-time schedule by restricting the networks to three of the four prime-time hours (7 P.M. to 11 P.M.). The results have been both encouraging and disappointing.

Most broadcasters lack the funds to engage in independent program production. Nevertheless, 11 independent production companies emerged from among the station owners, principally the largest. They produce first-run programs for the network market. These 11 producers together produce about 87 hours of programming a week. What is disappointing is the generally low level of their output. It began with game shows and has shifted to copycat family-situation shows. Hardly the elevating material hoped for by the FCC.

Another important rule of the game limits the number of broadcast media that can be owned by a single company. In March 1985 the FCC increased the number of stations that a single organization can own from the seven it had been to the current allowance of 12. If, however, the organization is owned

Table 5 Program Production Among TV Stations Owners, 1988

GROUP OWNER	PROGRAMMING PRODUCED (NO. HRS. PER WEEK)
Lorimar	25.0
Westinghouse	12.5
Tribune	11.0
Telmundo	9.0
Great American	8.0
Multi Media	7.5
Fox	6.0
Viacom International	4.5
Gannett	2.5
Gaylord	1.5
Total Hours	87.5

Source: H. Howard, *Cross Ownership*, National Association of Broadcasters, Washington, DC (1988).

by a Hispanic, a black, an American Indian, an Asiatic, or an Eskimo, then the number of broadcast stations allowed is 14. No group's total potential audience can exceed 25 percent of the nation's households (30 percent for minority groups listed above). This rule applies to AM and FM radio as well as to television.

As soon as this rule of "12 and 25 percent" went into effect, significant structural changes began to take place in the industry. Major companies were purchased and sold. General Electric bought the entire NBC organization, which, in addition to the network, included its extremely lucrative television stations. Capital Cities Broadcasting bought the entire ABC network, which also included very lucrative television stations. These networks have a history going back to the 1920s, when they had their start in radio. They were once proud, powerful, and independent media companies. Today they are mere subsidiaries of another organization.

Possibly to encourage shifting of network affiliation among broadcasters in a given market, the FCC established a ruling that a network's affiliation contract with a broadcaster must be renewed every two years.

The *"duopoly rule"* (which prohibits the ownership of more than one radio station and more than one television station, respectively, within the same market) is designed to preclude the domination of a market—or the political dominance of the local audience—by a single firm.

This is not an unreasonable concern. Working from the unlikely though possible premise that all media owners are scoundrels, one can at least have confidence that the conflicting interests of different owners will permit the public, should it wish, to obtain information regarding all sides of an issue with relative ease. In this respect, diverse ownership of media is important. However, a highly fractionated system that precludes the presence of large, though competing, media owners could lead to a different type of problem. Small size can result in timidity. It can deprive the nation of powerful media groups whose voice can be heard on the national scene. The media should have the power to stand up to the government, and to one another, if the public is to be served.

The media need organizations capable of resisting congressional indictments, affording the legal fees needed to bring issues to the Supreme Court, and making their voice heard on matters of principle. True, rich and influential organizations do not always rise to the occasion, but their *ability* to do so provides a necessary bulwark against an overbearing government bureaucracy or a media baron.

Some of the Results

The number of stations (or newspapers) owned by a corporation is no indication of the true size of the organization. This can be determined only by the size of the combined audience reached by the several media it owns. Until 1984, the FCC did not keep

a record of this information, nor did it design its policies on the
basis of the size of the audience reached. It relied only on the
number of media owned. This resulted in serious errors in policy
making. The new "12 and 25" rule rectified this oversight to some
extent.

Exactly how big, in terms of audience reached, *are* the large
media organizations? This question was the subject of a massive
computerized study directed by Herbert Howard on behalf of the
National Association of Broadcasters.

In this study, Howard found that there has been a substantial
increase in the "reach" of large group owners particularly as a
result of the new "12 and 25 percent" rule. This may seem
to some to be a cause for alarm. They see the consolidation
of broadcast stations into ever-larger companies as a threat to
the body politic. However, while media companies are growing
larger they are not becoming fewer. Twenty-three new television
groups were formed during this period of consolidation, resulting
in a slightly larger number of group owners than before. And
as long as the "duopoly rule" prevents consolidation within a
market, it is difficult to see any potential evil in consolidation,
especially when we consider the fact that broadcast station
owners, large and small, rarely produce programming. And
advertising is too competitive for even the larger companies to
exercise monopolistic pricing.

The muckraker playing armchair economist invariably points
to large and growing media companies to sound the alarm that
control over our collective mind is falling into fewer hands. The
big bugaboo is that someone will soon become Big Brother to the
nation. These alarmists profit from the magazine articles they sell
and the invitations they receive to address professional groups,
but there is no substance to their fears. They are simply ignorant
of the way in which mass media operate. The alarmists' ignorance
is shared by most academicians.

Even with today's relative freedom to increase one's media
holdings, only three groups have barely managed to reach more
than 20 percent of the nation's television audience through their

collection of broadcast stations. The largest, which reaches 24.5 percent of the nation's homes, achieves its share in large part through the assistance of cable systems that carry its signals beyond its local markets. Altogether only five groups reach as many as 15 percent and seven groups 10 percent of the nation's homes. And these include the stations owned by the three television networks that are located in America's largest metropolitan areas.

The big broadcast companies in 1988 were the Tribune Broadcasting Company, which reaches 24.5 percent of the nation's homes; and this, as already noted, is with the aid of two cable superstations. It is followed by the Capital Cities Broadcasting Company, which owns the ABC network (22.6 percent); General Electric, which owns the NBC network (21.1 percent); Fox (17.5 percent); CBS (17.3 percent); Gillett (12.6 percent); and Westinghouse (10.5 percent). By comparison, the smallest group owner in the United States—the Tri State Christian Broadcasting group, owning two broadcasting stations—reaches only 27,000 homes. There are altogether 184 group owners in the U.S. defined as companies owning more than one broadcast station.

In addition to broadcast stations, there has been an increasing consolidation between newspaper and television properties. This consolidation has been at the national level. At the local level, *within* America's cities—where there might be some concern regarding domination of a market and its possible effect on local politics—the newspaper-television connection has actually declined. Overall, there are 46 groups that combine ownership of newspapers and television stations. Locally, within the same city, there are 27 newspaper-television combinations. This represents a decline, since 1975, of 33 stations that had formerly been in joint ownership with a local newspaper.

Overall, regardless of the size of the market, approximately 27 percent of America's television stations are owned by companies that also own at least one newspaper. Here, too, there is

Table 6   Ten Largest TV Groups (ranked by net weekly circulation*)

TV GROUP	NO. TV STATIONS	PERCENTAGE OF U.S. HOUSEHOLDS	NO. RADIO STATIONS	NO. NEWS-PAPERS
Tribune	6	24.5	5	7
Capital Cities/ABC	8	22.6	16	8
GE/NBC	7	21.1	8	–
Fox	7	17.5	–	3
CBS	4	17.3	18	–
Gillette	12	12.6	–	–
Westinghouse	5	10.5	15	–
Cox†	8	9.7	11	20
Gannett‡	8	8.6	16	90
United/ChrisCraft	7	8.5	–	–

* Measures actual audience.

† Cox's 20 newspapers have a combined circulation of 1.3 million.

‡ Gannett's 90 newspapers have a combined circulation of 6 million.

Source: H. Howard, *Cross Ownership*, National Association of Broadcasters, Washington, DC (1988).

little cause for concern as long as these media are not both located in the same market. New acquisitions face divestiture if they happen to be in the same market. Thus, Murdoch's Fox Broadcasting had to sell off the *New York Post* when it acquired a New York television station. In any event, most major markets receive such a plethora of diverse media that there is almost no possibility to monopolize even local information.

In addition to newspaper-television cross-ownership, there are television companies that also own radio stations and cable systems. Five of the largest media companies own cable systems and 11 publish daily newspapers.

Whatever the outcome of changes in the ownership structure of broadcast stations and newspapers, radio stations and cable systems—and this is going on all the time—there is little real risk of domination. The reason lies in the fact that the electronic transmitting facilities are not at the center of mass communications in the United States. They are merely utilitics, conduits, the hardware of the system. The real power, to the extent that there is any, lies in the hands of those who produce the programming, the informants of the public. Later in our discussion we will investigate, up close, the ability to dominate a specific community or market.

Before leaving the issue of the industry's structure, it is important to note that there are no controls over statewide ownership; the FCC limitation on the ownership of broadcast facilities applies nationally and its "duopoly rule" applies within a market. A study made in the 1970s showed that in 28 states and the District of Columbia, there were communications companies with access to over 50 percent of the homes in the state.

Gatekeepers

Although the *owners* of communications facilities (newspapers and broadcasting stations) are strategically placed in the flow of information and entertainment, they rarely exercise this power on a day-to-day basis. Rather, they set overall policy and then rely on their staff (and on the major news services and the networks). In this respect, media owners are but one of several gatekeepers past whom the content of the mass media must flow. They exercise their power principally through the selection of station managers and newspaper editors, who, in turn, select the first line of gatekeepers, the producers, directors, reporters, and writers.

Yet group owners, those who own a number of media, have been referred to by their critics as "media barons." Historically, this title carries with it the somewhat sinister connotation of the muckraker era of the turn-of-the-century, when the collusive and antisocial behavior of a number of powerful industrialists shocked the nation into the enactment of the antitrust laws and the creation of the Federal Trade Commission.

But the proper operation of the mass media is far more important than the proper functioning of industrial enterprises. When information is withheld or distorted, it is difficult to galvanize public opinion into acting upon important social, economic, and political problems. Indeed, many of the early muckrakers relied on the press to bring the facts to the public.

It is argued that while, as a practical matter, news and entertainment are provided by "wholesalers" (that is, networks and wire services), the broadcaster and his subordinates are still free, if they so wish, to reject network programs, buy elsewhere, and edit the news according to their own point of view. Such critics are concerned that the present ownership structure of the communications system may have concentrated too much *political* power in the hands of the owners of the nation's broadcasting stations.

This is not a simple issue to resolve, for it is not an easy matter to determine to what extent an owner of media, even if he were the only owner of all local media (and such a monopoly exists nowhere in the United States), has the power to dominate the local political environment.

A first step in coming to grips with this issue is to measure the "reach" of a media owner's properties: the size of his actual audience. (We shall leave for the next chapter the even more problematic question of his ability to influence this audience.) This is not an easy task, since among other things it involves different types of media (newspapers, radio, and television) and each medium has its own statistical measures and its own definition of "audience."

The data that have to be assembled thus represent a combination of three different concepts of audience. In each instance, they represent the exposure that an owner can expect his media to receive at a given moment, but the concept of the "moment" also varies with the medium. The three concepts are: (1) the sales of a newspaper in an average day, which is less than its readership, since, on the average, more than one person reads each copy of a newspaper; (2) the number of homes tuned in to a radio station in an average week; and (3) the number of homes watching a television station in the course of a week. The use of these different measures is dictated by the type of statistics employed by each medium in its day-to-day operations.

Access to the Nation

As of June 1970, there were only 13 group owners in the United States who, through their ownership of press, radio, and television facilities, could at a given moment in time reach 5 percent or more of the nation's population. In 1988 this number had increased to 16 group owners. Apparently there is increasing competition at the top. And the top does not exceed 25 percent of the nation, except for the networks. A comparison of those among the top ten in 1970 with those at the top in 1988 reveals the absence of six companies. There does not seem to be much security in size.

Thus at the national level the evidence indicates that, while potential national influence accrues to any organization that commands the attention of over 5 percent of the nation, no group of media owners can effectively reach, much less sway, simply through its ownership of the facilities of mass communication.

Because, as producers of programming, the three networks reach virtually every home in the nation, the government's concern over the ownership of broadcasting stations is of little value or meaning. In effect, a large part of public regulation is founded upon a myth, the myth that the owners of broadcasting stations determine the content of the programs transmitted to the general public.

At the State Level

At the state level, things become a bit stickier. There are few, if any, statewide magazines or statewide dailies or statewide broadcasting stations; but a media group, properly assembled, can make a group owner's views a statewide affair.

Assume the worst, that a group owner at the state level lines up his media behind a specific candidate or issue. The effect of this coordinated effort will be limited to the extent that there are competing owners of comparable audience "reach" in the same state (assuming that they don't collude). The problem then is not only the size of the largest media owner's audience but the degree to which there are competing media organizations of equal size.

In Georgia, for example, at the time of the study the Cox Broadcasting Company reached an estimated 83 percent of the homes in the state, and the next largest media organization in that state reached only 17 percent of the homes. The state of Georgia did not lack media or media owners; it had 286 different media owners, but most of them were small, local operations or were located in surrounding states with broadcast or newspaper circulation in Georgia. As a consequence, there were no large media groups capable of countervailing the Cox organization. Under such circumstances, one must simply rely on the basic fairness of the dominant media owner and hope that he will not attempt to dominate. But this is a rather weak reed.

At the other extreme, it is probably equally bad to have a total absence of large media organizations at the state level. A highly localized structure would put a state's mass media at the mercy of public relations men. For without the investigative reporting staff that only large organizations can afford, the small newspapers and broadcasting stations have to reply on government press releases in their statewide coverage. This can be at least as dangerous as a single, dominant group owner.

Table 7 focuses on only those states in which were found very large media groups in a study made in 1970. Included in the table is the audience reach of the second-largest media group in that state. This affords some indication of the strength of the competition. In all, 28 states and the District of Columbia appear on this list. Attention is called to Minnesota, Nevada, and Rhode

Table 7   Dominant Media Owners, by State,* 1970

STATE	LARGEST GROUP OWNER	PROPORTION OF HOMES REACHED LARGEST OWNER*	NEXT IN SIZE
Arizona	Central Newspapers, Inc.	54%	45%
Connecticut	WTIC	59	20
Delaware	Wilmington Journal	55	43
Dist. of Columbia	Post–Newsweek Stns.	96	74
Georgia	Cox Broadcasting Company	83	17
Idaho	Bonneville Int'l. Corp.	57	25
Illinois	Patterson Family	68	40
Iowa	Cowles-Ridder	65	48
Kentucky	WHAS, Inc.	68	23
Maine	Guy Gannett Bcstg.	79	52
Maryland	Hearst Corp.	58	45
Massachusetts	Group W–Westinghouse Bcstg. Co.	62	60
Michigan	Evening News Assn.	54	28
Minnesota	Cowles-Ridder	100	29
Montana	Garryowen Stns.	52	38
Nebraska	Herald Corp.	60	38
Nevada	Southwestern Operating Company	100	26
New Hampshire	Group W–Westinghouse Bcstg. Co.	60	36
North Dakota	WDAY Stns. Forum Publishing Co.	53	47
Oklahoma	WKY T.V. System, Inc.	69	30
Oregon	Newhouse S.I.	89	29
Pennsylvania	Group W–Westinghouse Bcstg. Co.	51	46
Rhode Island	Providence Jrnl. Co.	100	56
South Dakota	Midcontinent Bcstg. Co.	61	40
Tennessee	Scripps-Howard Bcstg. Co.	51	24
Utah	Glassman A.L.	98	68
Virginia	Richmond Newspapers	50	33
Wisconsin	Journal Co.	75	27
Wyoming	Frontier Bcstg. Stns.	53	38

*Those reaching 50 percent or more of the homes in the state.

Source: M. H. Seiden & Associates, Inc., *Special Study* (FCC Docket 18110; 1971).

Island, where the largest group owner reached every home in the state. In Nevada and Minnesota, the runner-up was not very strong. It reached less than 30 percent of the audience.

Viewed from a different perspective, it is probably of some national significance to know which media owners had a significant position in more than one state. Reducing our cutoff points to a 25-percent reach, an analysis of the data shows that there were four multistate group owners, each of whom had access to over 25 percent of the homes in five different states. They were: ABC, Cowles-Ridder, Newhouse, and Scripps-Howard. Three corporations each had this position in four states. They were CBS, NBC (RCA), and Westinghouse. Similarly, four corporations held a dominant position in three states. They were: Bonneville International (the Mormon Church), Capital Cities Broadcasting, Harriscope Stations, and RKO (General Tire). Beyond this point there were 15 groups and corporations playing a dominant role in each of two different states, and 60 groups or corporations with a more than 25-percent share of the audience each in just one state.

It should be noted that although the data indicate that there is some ground for concern regarding media ownership at the state level, there are no rules for media ownership within a state.

Barons in the Marketplace

The third and the most controversial level of concern regarding private ownership of the mass media is in the cities. For some inexplicable reason, the cities have been of greater concern to the federal regulatory authorities than the states. The "duopoly rule" (you can't own more than one property in each type of medium), which applies only to the cities, seems adequate in itself as a control over domination by single owner. Nevertheless, the FCC persists in playing around with its rules at this level. One of the complicating features of the city or market is the definition of its size.

Among the most common definitions of "market" is the government's Standard Metropolitan Statistical Area (SMSA). This is a grouping of contiguous counties in and around a city that forms a market based on the location of the population. There is, however, a fairly long time lag in the adjustment of the SMSA definition of a market to shifts in the population; but more important, as we shall see, it is not always an accurate reflection of the economics of the marketplace.

The political jurisdiction of the city is sometimes employed to define the market, but this, too, lacks an economic foundation, being based on law and historical precedence.

The American Research Bureau (ARB), a private audience-research firm, developed the concept of ADI, or area of dominant influence. This is a communications-oriented concept now in wide use, in which every one of the more than 3,000 counties in the United States is assigned to some market based on the location of the television stations that command the majority of the viewing hours reported for that county. Altogether, there are about 204 ADI markets in the continental United States. The ADI concept is the most valid basis for defining integrated geographic and economic units for the purpose of analyzing mass communications since it defines a market from the standpoint of the advertiser.

Commuter mobility, discussed in the last chapter, has led to the development of suburban satellite communities around the urban core and the decentralization of retail sales through widely scattered shopping centers. Consequently, the communications media have become the binding force in today's retail markets— which underlies the birth of the ADI concept. Although based on the television audience, it is a concept now being used in planning newspaper advertising as well.

The importance of the definition for public policy lies in the fact that the larger the size of the market, the greater the number of competing media and competing media owners attributed to the market. Thus the mistaken use of the SMSA definition by the FCC led the commission, in 1969, to adopt a policy that virtually wiped out the multi-million-dollar Boston Herald Traveler Corporation.

The Boston SMSA consists of just four counties. However, the Boston television signals serve an ADI of 16 counties, including seven in New Hampshire and one each in Connecticut and Vermont.

By relying on the antiquated SMSA concept, the FCC credited Boston with only five television signals. Under the ADI concept, the market originated eight television signals and received 16 more from adjoining markets. Similarly, the FCC credited Boston with only 19 radio signals on the SMSA concept, while the ADI concept credited it with originating 68 signals. The Boston ADI was also served by 41 dailies (of which each of 17 had a daily circulation in five figures) and 140 weeklies.

Overall, the Boston ADI has access to 257 media originating in that market, owned by 190 different groups, individuals, or corporations. The FCC data speak of only 27 media: five television signals, 19 radio signals, and three dailies. It is because of these erroneous data that the FCC felt that the Boston market could use greater diversification of media ownership and, as a result, withdrew the license of WHDH-TV, whose parent company also owned a major Boston newspaper and radio station. This led to the collapse of the entire enterprise, reducing rather than increasing the number of media available to the Boston public.

It should be noted that today the FCC employs the ADI as its market framework.

The Role of Size

The greater the number of large group owners in the market, the more intense the competition. But a person located in almost any part of a market will be reached by many more media owners than just those able to reach more than a quarter or half of the population. For example, a person living in a market may or may not be reached by one of the major owners. It all depends on where in the market he lives and works, for there are numerous other media and media owners in the market, though they may cover much smaller sections of the city.

The center of the market is probably the area of greatest overlap of media and media owners. Generally speaking, the farther one travels from the center of the market, the fewer the alternative "voices" available—but also the thinner the population density. In this respect, the number of different media correlates with density of the population. This is understandable: A larger population attracts a larger number of advertisers, who, in turn, are able to support a larger number of media.

The largest media owner, in terms of market distribution, used to be Samuel Newhouse, whose 21 newspapers, five television stations, and three radio stations provided him with a substantial share (over 25 percent) of 11 different markets. By 1988, Newhouse had sold off many of his media assets.

All in all, in 1970 there were 236 media owners with access to 25 percent or more of the homes in each of one or more markets in the United States. But, for reasons we discuss in the next chapter, the situation is now in a state of flux.

For a well-rounded view of what concerns the government (FCC and Justice Department) in matters of media ownership, we must also note their current worry over cross-media ownership; that is, ownership of different media by a single company serving the same market. This is the issue that did in the Boston Herald Traveler Corporation.

This concern on the part of the government is oddly timed. Cross-media ownership involving radio and newspapers is now at its lowest level. This is true both in absolute numbers of radio stations, as well as relative to the total number of radio stations. Thus, in 1950, 472 radio stations were owned by newspapers. This was 22.6 percent of the total. By 1988, the number had fallen to below 300 stations and was by then less than 1 percent of the industry.

In the case of television stations, the current situation cannot be compared with 1950, since there were only 97 commercial television stations in the entire country at that time and there are 1,400 in 1988. But proportionate to the total, newspaper ownership of television broadcasting has also been declining.

The government's concern relates particularly to the big cities and their major television stations. But, by the government's count, there are only 43 cities left in which there is more than one major newspaper owner, yet every major city has three or more competing television stations (also based on FCC definitions). Judging from their own data, cross-media ownership in the cities is not the nation's most pressing problem in the field of mass communications, regardless of the concept of the size of the market one uses.

Concern over the size of the media group is really concern over the size of the audience that it will be influencing. Implicit here is the belief that the media necessarily, willy-nilly, influence the audience. But do they? Equally perplexing is the government's view that one needs to *own* media in order to have access to the public. Do not the employees and persons who *rent* the media by buying space (newspaper) or time (broadcasting) also have an opportunity to reach the public? The important question, of course, is the extent to which owners and renters of media in fact possess the ability to influence the audience. As we have noted earlier, there is considerable evidence to the contrary.

4 Upheaval[1]

The Golden Age

Mass communications in America is now going through a major upheaval. It would not be an exaggeration to say that it is the most significant period of change in mass communications since the advent of television.

New technology is moving into the marketplace. Much of it is mutually exclusive, so that several new technologies perform the same function but in radically different ways. Economics and standardization require that only a few survive. These technological changes will not only perform today's functions differently, they will provide entirely new services that will transform the way Americans conduct their businesses and run their households.

The process referred to earlier as "creative destruction" has accompanied these new technologies. Several corporate giants have already been reduced to marginal players and new companies have emerged who may be tomorrow's leaders. But the process has just begun. Corporate upheavals will continue for several years, until technological change and public policy stabilize.

Examples of this process of industrial change already noted include the disappearance of RCA, the first American company in the field of electronics and mass communications. It was the parent of the NBC network and formerly one of America's leading manufacturers of radios, television sets, records, and allied equipment. It was bought in its entirety by General Electric. Today RCA is simply one of GE's subsidiaries. Similarly, the ABC network, a household name, was bought by Capital Cities Broadcasting, which few Americans have ever heard of. Giant advertising agencies, too, have been swallowed up, in this case, by foreign companies.

On the other hand, the Tribune Corporation, a relative unknown outside the industry, has today become one of the media companies with the greatest "reach." Through its television and newspaper properties it reaches over one-quarter of all American homes. But that was in 1988. The ongoing reorganization of the industry may even now have seen the creation of newer media giants with a still greater reach. Industry dominance is no longer a guarantee of stability or longevity.

At one time the three television networks had the greatest reach by virtue of the fact that their programming served virtually every market and reached into every home. But that has already changed. After decades in which the three networks accounted for 100 percent of all television viewing, their share of television viewing had, by 1989, declined to about 58 percent and their share of all broadcast advertising had dropped to 35 percent.

At a press conference in May 1988, the president of the NBC television network reported that television in America is making a transition to pay-TV. He described a system in which the viewer pays for watching *what* he wants, *when* he wants, as opposed to the old advertiser-supported free viewing of predetermined fare on a fixed schedule.

As he pointed out, there were already 23 major cable networks offering special viewing packages for an additional fee and over 40,000 home video stores in the United States renting and selling films and special tapes directly to the consumer. At the time he spoke, half of all homes in America were served by cable and VCRs, 32 percent by pay-TV. By the early 1990s, he forecast that 70 percent of American homes will receive television through cable; and he might have added VCR as well. Television will, he estimates, produce about $43 billion in revenues annually, as compared to today's advertising revenue of $25 billion.

With cash flow of this magnitude, it is clear that the old way of doing business, based on advertising revenue, will be secondary. New modes of pricing and financing program production and program distribution will evolve. A corporation that sticks to the old methods will become as obsolete as the silent movie.

The NBC network was already buying cable systems rather than risk being rendered obsolete by relying exclusively on the present broadcasting system. In operating as a broadcast network, NBC distributes it programs via satellite to hundreds of local broadcasting stations, which then rebroadcast the network's programs free to the local viewer over the airwaves. The network shares with the broadcaster some of the advertising revenue obtained from the national advertisers and the broadcaster inserts local advertising around the network's program.

If the network didn't have to share its national advertiser revenue with the broadcaster and, on top of that, if the public paid for programs it wanted, then television programming would be much more lucrative. It is apparent why the president of NBC felt that, financially, the golden age of television was first arriving.

The social implications of these changes are also meaningful. Viewers will call in those programs that they want through a pay-TV-type operation or select them from among several channels provided by cable. Each channel would specialize in a *type* of program, much as does radio today. The mass media of today will have given way to "boutique" programming. The public's ability to program for themselves will alter what is today considered "mass culture." Magazines underwent these changes in the 1970s with the demise of such powerful nationally distributed publications as *Life, Look, Collier's,* and the *Saturday Evening Post.* While they died, highly specialized and even local magazines multiplied and thrived.

With a television system based on consumer payment for programs, independent producers will be able to compete for access to the viewer. The customer will be the consumer and not, as in the past, the advertiser or a company that controls the gateway to the public—as have the networks over the years. The new technologies are bringing, in their wake, radical changes in the way of doing business.

This, however, is but the tip of the iceberg. What the president of NBC failed to consider was the possibility that cable might not be the vehicle of the future.

The New Competitor

Looming over the television industry as we know it today is another industry that, itself, has undergone radical change in the past decade. Once the largest corporation in the world, the American Telephone and Telegraph Corporation, otherwise known as AT&T or "Ma Bell," used to be a regulated monopoly controlling much of the nation's telephone system. The federal government broke up this monopoly in the 1980s. Local telephone service all over America is now the business of several regional companies spun off from AT&T. The mother company is today restricted to long-distance calls. New companies, such as MCI and Sprint, were allowed to compete with AT&T for long-distance telephone business in order to reduce dependence on public regulation.

Like television sets, telephones are found in almost every American household. The telephone industry employs over 660,000 people and services 220 million telephones that handle

1.3 billion conversations daily. Overall, the telephone industry's annual revenue is about $90 billion, or more than twice that of the television communications industry, even when we include in the latter the $12 billion paid by Americans for their cable service.

Today the telephone industry is itself undergoing major technological change. These changes are about to bring it into conflict with the existing television communications system.

Everyone is familiar with the copper wires buried under our streets and strung on telephone polls. These copper wires carry a few hundred telephone conversations and no television. They are currently being replaced, nationwide, with *fiber optics*. A single fiber-optic strand can carry 24,000 telephone conversations or 20 video channels. And this is well below its ultimate potential. The telephone industry had, by 1988, already connected all major metropolitan areas with fiber. Over 3 million miles of fiber *cable* have already been installed in the United States.

These cables contain anywhere from six to 72 strands of fiber. A single cable with 72 strands of glass fiber can carry 1.7 million conversations or an almost unlimited number of television channels, *simultaneously*. The new capacity being installed is enormous. And the pace of the change can be judged by the fact that in the state of New Jersey alone there is already more fiber optic in use than in all of Europe.

The telephone companies will soon be in a position to deliver to the American home not only telephone and data services but also dozens of channels of television—something they could not do before. This poses a threat to the television communications industry. The telephone companies will want to recover their extraordinary investment in new physical plants, and television would be a lucrative addition to their revenue. Telephones are in service, on the average, only 30 minutes a day in the average American home. To fully utilize the potential in fiber calls for its use in the transmission of television. Television viewing consumes an average of seven hours a day in the average American home.

But there is an important difference between the telephone companies and existing media companies. The telephone companies can provide a unique service that the others are not in a position to offer. The telephone companies can provide a switchboard service generally referred to as an interchange. This allows a subscriber to interact with the communicator or to call in his choice of video, voice, or hard-copy facsimile from a specific supplier. It presents the opportunity for *universal interactive television communication*.

The telephone companies would thus be able to perform all the functions of today's broadcaster and cable television system, and much more. The door is open to interactive and visual education, financial services, medical services, and sales. Also capable of being facilitated are independent video productions, alternative or supplementary school services, video "snapshot" transfer, interpersonal computer services, audience polling, merchandising, telemetry, alarm services, and more.

Currently the telephone companies can't enter these businesses because they are all *common carriers*. That means that they can, by law, provide only the service of carrying information for others. They cannot market their own programs or their own information. Today this means serving as a carrier of other people's conversations, other people's data, facsimile, and video signals. They have to stand ready to serve any subscriber who is willing to pay the fee.

It might be wise to keep this arrangement and allow competing suppliers of these services to share the common carrier's access to the public.

On the other hand, the government might allow the telephone companies to be information suppliers as well. This might follow from the argument that cable companies can also provide fiber-optic service to the home. They need only switch to this new technology. As a result, the telephone companies would no longer have a monopoly. There would then not be as strong an argument for restricting telephone company activity to that of passive common carrier. Telephone companies would, however, still have the great advantage of their switching capability. They can interconnect everyone everywhere through their interexchange facilities.

Whereas this might seem to represent a conflict between cable systems and the telephone companies, the real losers will be those who invested in television broadcasting stations. They will all be rendered obsolete when American homes are served by fiber optics.

If, however, the telephone companies remain common carriers, broadcasters could continue to be the local program source, but they will have to pay the common carrier or the cable system in order to be carried into the homes of local viewers. And what will they have to offer? It is almost certain that under these new arrangements broadcasters would no longer receive payment to broadcast network programs. The network and non-network program producers would be selling their wares directly through the carrier to the television audience.

The only salvation for the broadcasters would be to become the local program producers, providing local programming of the type now provided by radio. If they took advantage of the many channels available on fiber, they could offer separate local channels for music, sports, news, financial advice and information, children's programs, and homemakers' programs— leaving expensive entertainment to regional or national networks that deal directly with the carrier or the public. In this way the local broadcaster would become a program producer and obtain support from local advertisers who, even today, account for lion's share of advertising.

Or will the government make the tragic error of trying to protect an obsolete technology? This happened before, when cable first made its appearance. The effect is apparent in the statistics. In 1980, when cable was regulated by the federal government, it took 14 years to reach 15 million homes, or 20 percent of the nation. By 1989, following the government's abandonment of cable regulation, cable service reached 48 million homes, or 54 percent of the nation. The government had been quashing consumer demand. The government must decide whom it serves, the public or the broadcaster.

But our story doesn't end here. The cable and telephone industries are as threatened as the broadcaster by still another technology that is even now trying to take over the market. They can all be rendered obsolete by this newcomer.

Threat from Outer Space

Space satellites have been a part of the American communications scene for almost a decade. The public is familiar with this technology because of the NASA programs. But not many people realize that almost all television received in the American home today, whether through the airwaves or through a cable system, arrived after a journey through space, where it bounced off a domestic space satellite. For several years now, all the television networks have been providing their programs to their affiliated broadcast stations via satellite. The large cable networks also receive many of their signals through satellite transmission. This is a sleeping giant, since satellites represent the seed of an entirely new approach to television distribution.

Television signals need not go through a local broadcast station or through a cable system; they can come straight from outer space directly into the home—with earth-shaking consequences for conventional communications systems.

In order for the satellite's signal to reach the American household directly, all that is required is a special antenna that costs not much more than a year's subscription to a cable system.

The fact is, nearly two million homes have already purchased this antenna and, for a while, they were receiving the program fare of all the major cable systems as well as the networks. They were tapping into the interconnection between the program source and the distributors without paying a fee. (To counteract this growing interception, the cable networks encoded their signals.) This is referred to as Direct Broadcast Satellite service. With it, neither cables nor broadcast stations are necessary. The only limiting factor is the number of transponders for rent or sale in outer space.

Today, nine companies have 26 U.S. domestic satellites in orbit. Together they provide 524 transponders, each of which can carry a single television channel. Of these, 402 are in what is called the C-band, which requires the very large dishes one sees at most television broadcasting facilities. The other 122 transponders are in what is called the Ku-band, which operates on a higher frequency and higher power and requires small antennas, the type associated with direct-to-the-home broadcasting. The price of these antennas is falling as demand increases, and newer, more compact models will soon be available.

A significant crossroad for commercial satellites will be reached in 1995, when nearly 70 percent of the C-band and 30 percent of the Ku-band transponders will require replacement. They have, under the existing state of the art, an average life expectancy of ten years. By then it is estimated that the United States will require the launching of about 40 new commercial space satellites. Worldwide, the estimate is for a need for 145 satellite launchings.

The changing character of mass communications as we enter the twenty-first century can be glimpsed by the fact that the Soviet Union's new commercial launch agency, Glavkosmos, offers to launch new satellites for $30 million, which is about half the price charged for NASA launches. And Communist China's Great Wall Industries Corporation says that it will beat anyone's price for space launchings. It claims it is negotiating with 40 firms, most of them American.

The great advantage of satellite over cable and fiber is its multi-point transmission abilities and the ease and low cost of reconfiguring the signal's distribution to meet changing demands. Fiber's advantage is signal quality and signal security. It doesn't require that the signal be coded to keep it private.

Currently fiber optics is the main challenge to direct-to-the-home communications via satellite. While fiber is being installed at a rapid rate, there has also been an explosive growth in the use of Ku-band by private business. It has proven to be a convenient and cost-effective method for daily data and video communications for companies with businesses spread all over the country. It has reduced corporate communications costs by up to 40 percent.

The ease and relatively low cost of satellite use has encouraged nearly 150 broadcasters to invest in mobile satellite news vehicles that allow them to broadcast through a space satellite from wherever news and sporting events of regional or national interest occur in their "territory." These broadcasts are shared via satellite with other broadcasters who belong to their satellite news network or satellite news cooperative. There were, in 1989, at least nine news networks or cooperatives, and there appears to be a growing awareness of the potential in this technology. Thus, a specialty firm focusing on news for people over 50 years of age was established in 1989. It provides its network of 124 subscribing broadcast stations with features and news aimed at this audience for inclusion in the broadcaster's news programs. The possibilities for easy entry into the mass-communications field through satellites has barely been tapped.

Rupert Murdoch's News Corporation, which founded the Fox Television Network in the United States, established in February 1989 a satellite network in Britain called Sky Television. It offers four channels that can be received at the subscriber's home direct from the satellite. To encourage subscriptions the company offers its service along with an antenna at an all-inclusive charge of $7.20 a week. For most Britons, this service doubles the number of channels available.

Ironically, Sky Television's first major customer was a large cable system. It is ironic because cable technology is assisting the establishment of a satellite service whose direct-to-the-home communications capability may eventually render cable obsolete.

The principal problem facing a satellite network such as Sky Television is the dearth of special antennas in place. A key to the successful establishment of direct-to-the-home broadcasting is the development of a cheap antenna. Barring that, antennas should be leased or even provided free. The antenna is far cheaper than the cost of putting in cable. Currently, cable has a sales advantage in that the number of channels it can deliver exceeds the number available through subscription to a satellite service. With time, this is likely to be offset by the development of advertiser-supported, satellite-delivered television that will doubtless develop to replace the mass market that was until now delivered by the networks and their affiliates.

The Cable Phenomenon

The evolution of community antenna television into today's cable systems is discussed elsewhere in this book. The extraordinary success of unregulated cable has brought it to the forefront of the industry's options for the future. The major operators in the communications industry are unconcerned by the competition offered by cable so long as they can buy their way into what conventional wisdom considers to be the wave of the future. The question is, has this medium been oversold? The brief review, above, of the new possibilities clearly indicates that this is not a closed issue. It will be a decade before the results are in.

In the meantime, while the other actors are waiting in the wings, cable television has grown to 8,000 systems serving over 48 million households. In the process, these cables pass a total of 74 million homes, theoretically allowing for a potential growth of up to 50 percent without further major investment in physical plant. This will require better programming and aggressive selling. That means that the theoretical limit, given today's investment in cable, is to reach about 75 percent of America.

As already noted, the cable industry currently earns $12 billion a year from subscription fees. In view of the declining possibility for new cable franchises, cable television's growth through an increase in the number of subscribers appears to be under $18 billion. Radical rate increases are not likely, as they would be counterproductive. They would almost certainly bring back some form of regulation or spur the entry of competing technologies.

A possibility for future growth is "pay cable," in which the subscriber pays for a package of channels that offer special types of programming, such as feature films, sports, or music. These special packages have, to date, been bought by only half of all cable customers. And, finally, there is advertising.

Advertising seems to offer the least potential for growth of cable revenue. It is estimated currently to total a little over $1 billion a year. The public believes that cable is an alternative to advertiser-supported programming. It would resent heavy advertising on cable. It is also hard to imagine cable, with its fractionated viewing, providing the advertiser with the simplicity and efficiency of broadcast audiences.

The advertising that has gotten on cable has accompanied what is called "narrowcasting," as opposed to broadcasting. This is advertising aimed at a narrow market, such as teenagers or sports fans. It appears on MTV (Music Television) or ESPN (Sports Network), which cater to these markets. These "networks" are transmitted to subscribing cable systems all over the nation through satellite transmission.

The production of a continuous supply of original entertainment programs lies beyond the ability of cable systems. They don't generate enough cash. Even the largest multiple system is still not large enough. Thus, the three major networks spend $6 billion a year on programming—equal to half the total income of the entire cable industry. The networks spend over $100 million a year on program development; a single episode for an hour-long series costs $1.2 million to produce. This is more than cable systems can budget on a regular basis.

Even if cable companies did spend a proportionate amount on program production, they would still not be in a position to sell advertisers a block of local viewers as broadcasters had done in the past. The very nature of cable television is to provide a multiplicity of channels and program alternatives. Their audience is thus too fractionated to sell to as a reliable mass audience. There could not be the same advertiser support for their programming as that obtained by the broadcast networks.

Cable systems lack the economic incentive to become major program producers since they earn their subscription fees regardless of whether or not they provide programs. Ironically, cables' success is eroding the advertising revenue that supports the networks. Yet the broadcast networks are the cable systems' principal source of programming. The cable systems' success may very well do in its principal source of sustenance.

Program in a Can

No one paid much attention to it at the beginning. The first videocassette recorders sold for $1,200. Prerecorded tapes cost $70 or more and were available only in the major cities. The VCR looked like a rich man's toy in 1980. At the time, there weren't even one million VCRs in use in the United States.

By the end of the decade better machines were selling for under $400, selling at the rate of 12 million a year. More than half of all American households had one. Prerecorded tapes were renting for as low as 99 cents and were available almost everywhere through over 40,000 outlets nationwide.

It would be an understatement to say that the mass-communications industry was taken by surprise. At first, the movie studios even opposed its growth. They saw it as a threat to their success at the box office. But it very soon became apparent that they were going to earn more from the VCR than from the movie theater.

By 1988, receipts from the sale and rental of prerecorded tapes exceeded theater box-office revenues. In less than a decade the VCR produced an annual gross revenue in excess of $8 billion, equal to two-thirds of the gross revenue of the cable industry.

And the cable owners had to slug it out for nearly 30 years and invest an immense sum in physical plant to arrive at what is today considered their current success. The prerecorded tape business, on the other hand, required almost no capital investment in physical plant.

As an example of what the VCR did for the movie studios, Paramount's film *Top Gun* earned for the studio $82 million at the box office and brought in $40 million from the sale of its prerecorded tape. Its earnings from the prerecorded tape alone would have made it one of the top ten earners in the year it was released. The great bulk of films that are financially unsuccessful at the box office often recover the studio's investment through their sale to the VCR market.

The prerecorded tape has become big business. About 200 new titles are released by some 140 home video companies every month! Over 110 million prerecorded videocassettes are purchased by retailers in a single year.

In the process of assuming its place as part of the mass-communications industry, the VCR has made serious inroads into the audiences and the economic support of both cable television and broadcaster: first, because the ability to rent movies cheaply undercuts the public's interest in pay-TV; second, because the networks' audiences are diverted from the traditional prime-time viewing by their use of prerecorded tapes; and third, because the VCR gives the viewer the ability to record programs delivered by cable or by the broadcaster and then to "zap" the commercials when watching the program at a later time. All this undercuts the advertising support of broadcast television. It could be an even greater threat to their advertising support if the prerecorded tapes carried their own advertisements, though the advertiser would still face the threat of being "zapped," but perhaps at a lower cost per thousand.

Despite its rapid growth, the influence of home video is only beginning to be felt. Coming out of nowhere and blossoming into a multibillion-dollar industry in only a few years, home video is a

case cxample of what is in store for us in the last decade of the
twentieth century. The rush to cable by investors and consumers
may well prove to have been a short-term strategy. The results
have yet to come in from fiber optics and space satellites. And
who knows what lasers and compact discs have in store for us?
Or what will follow from high definition television, HDTV, whose
picture is as sharp as a color slide? There may be at this very
minute an undreamed-of new technology waiting to spring on us
from someone's laboratory. Ever hear of holography?

5 Political Power

Agnewism

When, in 1970, American Vice President Spiro Agnew denounced the media, nearly everyone accepted his basic premise that the media had the power to mold public opinion. Almost no one bothered to investigate the truthfulness of this basic premise, least of all the media professionals, who probably found this imputation of power a source of pride. Instead, the question that was debated was whether the media were being fair in their use of this power.

Molding public opinion can be interpreted in one of two ways: that the public is malleable because it accepts what it is told; or that it sits in judgment on the information it receives and uses it to form its opinions. The distinction is critical. It is the difference between imputing ignorance or intelligence to the audience. Agnew's use of the term "molding" implied that the audience is malleable and ignorant—otherwise why be so concerned? Misrepresentation of the facts is easily dealt with.

Eventually, the truth will out (as Agnew himself was destined to learn).

Agnew expressed the administration's indignation at being subjected to criticism, fearing that the public's attitude had been prejudiced. But unjustified as the criticism might or might not have been, that administration and all subsequent administrations certainly did not lack access to the American mind. Virtually all of the media were at its disposal in order to debate the issues. Indeed, in his first 18 months in office President Nixon appeared on television as many times as presidents Eisenhower, Kennedy, and Johnson combined.[1] It did not help him.

In addition, the administration has at its disposal the enormous power of the federal bureaucracy. In Dale Minor's *The Information of War*, the public information operations of the executive branch in the 1970s were said to cost the taxpayer $400 million a year, more than double the cost of newsgathering by the two major U.S. wire services, the three major television networks, and the ten largest newspapers in the United States combined.[2]

In addition to Nixon's unlimited ability to make his views known to the public on his own terms—by commandeering the nation's entire broadcasting establishment and by being able to put into the field a veritable army of public relations men—his critics in the news media had a public relations problem of their own. An ABC network poll following Agnew's attack on the broadcast media found that 51 percent of the public agree with him that the media were biased, 16 percent were uncertain, and 33 percent disagreed.[3] This is not a picture of a public that is unaware of the quality of its news sources. Why, then, were Agnew and the president so upset about their treatment by the mass media?

With time, it has become apparent that they could have been concerned that the probing of reporters might reveal what *was* eventually revealed: the unseemly behavior that led to Agnew's resignation and forced Nixon to resign. But Nixon's known attitude toward the mass media tends to support the likelihood that he truly accepted the myth of the public credulousness, that, as he saw it, the mass media determined his personal popularity and the success or failure of his policies.

Getting the Facts

Congressman Robert Eckhardt (Dem., Texas) made a rare attempt to test Agnew's assertion that the "liberal eastern establishment" were implacably hostile to the Nixon Administration. He took upon himself the task of surveying the editorial policies of 154 newspapers and their views on a number of key political issues that preoccupied the Nixon Administration in the 1968–70 period.

The greatest opposition to administration policies, it was found, came from the Midwestern papers, not those in the ("liberal") East. Perhaps equally surprising, the greatest support came from the Western papers rather than the Southern. As a matter of fact, Southern newspaper responses were not at all different from responses of newspapers as a whole.

G. Harold Carswell's nomination to the Supreme Court had little editorial support, even in the South; the Eastern press was not the radical liberal monolith that the vice president thought it was; and any opposition that there was in the press to administration policies was not part of a liberal conspiracy. The administration, when it lost a majority of the large newspapers on an issue, lost by and large its basic supporters. Two-thirds of the nation's newspapers *endorsed* Nixon–Agnew in 1968, but 69 percent *opposed* Carswell.

The Eckhardt study showed that the newspapers are Republican-oriented, but apparently they are not slaves to the party and its leaders' policies. They can and do provide a platform for diverse editorial positions on questions of important national policy.

The Republican Party received the endorsement of the majority of the newspapers in every election since 1932, with the exception of the year 1964. Their margin has been two or three to one over the Democratic candidate, and in terms of the newspapers' circulation, rather than the number of newspapers, it was often higher.

The survey also revealed that both in the Northeast, whose "liberal press" was attacked so vehemently by the vice president, as well in the traditionally Democratic South, the Republican presidential candidate generally had the support of the majority of the newspapers.

In attacking the press for allegedly failing to support administration policies, Agnew clearly implied that the absence of public support on some issues must necessarily mean that the media were failing him; in other words, that the public's mind had not been properly conditioned by them.

The difficulties facing the Nixon Administration were thus being blamed on the public's "informers"—that is, the media—rather than on the events that made the electorate unhappy: the depressing, spirit-rending stories of over a decade of war, death, riots, and finally corruption. These were not the fault of the media, unless one would argue that the public should not be informed.

What could have caused Agnew (and Nixon) to be so misled? The evidence indicates that the idea that the media are intrinsically powerful (i.e., influential) probably is one of the few ideas that the media have truly been able to impose on the public. Writing in his own newspaper, Richard Harwood, a managing editor of the *Washington Post*, quoted Walter Lippmann to the effect that there is a "realization in this country that the power to shape the mass mind . . . has fallen into the hands of a very small number of men and women [journalists]. . . . They are the new Popes in their influence on the secular mind in America."[4] Similarly, Fred Friendly, formerly head of CBS News and then head of the Columbia University School of Journalism, called television a "potent magic wand."[5] This type of self-inflating professionalism is analogous to Hollywood's penchant for making films of the lives of entertainers or the Catholic Church's canonization of clerics. Professional narcissism is more responsible for concern regarding the power of the media than their ability truly to manipulate the public mind.

A close look at specific media in specific markets where political power can be suspected was undertaken by the author a number of years ago. It focused on the question of whether or not the media mold public opinion. A cross-sectional view of findings in three cities follows.[6]

Chicago: The Big City Baron

Chicago, then and still the third-largest city in the nation, has that combination of circumstances that calls attention to the role of the mass media. It then had a powerful mayor-boss, Richard Daley, but paradoxically it was also one of the few major cities with two strong competing media groups: McCormick-Patterson and Field Enterprises (Marshall Field).

The McCormick-Patterson group owned a local AM and FM radio station, a popular local television station (WGN), and two of Chicago's four principal newspapers: the *Chicago Tribune*, which had a morning circulation within the city of Chicago of 305,000, and *Chicago Today*, which had an evening circulation within the city of 287,000. Together the corporation's two newspapers reached 51 percent of the households in the city every day. When its other media were included, the McCormick-Patterson group probably reached every home in Chicago in the course of an average week.

Field Enterprises' holdings in Chicago also consisted of two newspapers—the *Chicago Sun-Times* (338,000 within the city) and the *Chicago Daily News* (245,000)—and a small local television station (WFLD). Like McCormick-Patterson, Field Enterprises' two newspapers reached almost half of Chicago's households. However, in the course of an average week it was not as likely that Field's media reached most of the local citizenry because of the relatively smaller size of its television audience.

The three network television and radio stations in Chicago were also dominant, in that they reached every Chicago home in the course of an average week. But there were also a great number of smaller media in Chicago: 402 different media originate in the greater Chicago area, owned by 224 different companies or groups, and another 80 different media, owned by 55 different owners, enter the market from outside.[7] However, with the exception of network television and radio stations and a number of nationally distributed magazines, none shared anywhere near the popularity of the McCormick-Patterson or Field Enterprises groups. And the exceptions didn't really count, since network-owned media as well as nationally distributed magazines rarely become embroiled in local politics.

To test the influence of the McCormick-Patterson group in Chicago, the author made an analysis of its political endorsements during the local primary and subsequent municipal elections in 1967. It was found that of 56 local political contests the two McCormick-Patterson newspapers endorsed opposing candidates in half of them. Both of the McCormick-Patterson newspapers, however, supported Mayor Daley.

Of the candidates endorsed by the *Chicago Tribune*, only 50 percent won in the primaries and 56 percent in the elections. The other newspaper of the McCormick-Patterson group, *Chicago Today*, did better: 82 percent of the candidates it endorsed won in the primaries and 80 percent in the elections. With the exception of Mayor Daley, these media went in different directions and scored differently as a result.

The election of endorsed candidates should be interpreted with care. It does not necessarily prove media influence. Did the media succeed in selling the public on those candidates or did it merely succeed in reading the public mind? Mayor Daley is a case in point. Was his success from 1955 on to be attributed to the support he obtained from the media, to his opponents' ineptitude, to his own political organization's ability to turn out the vote, or to his own ability? These are not simple questions. It is almost certain, however, that the dominant media were not the basis of Daley's political power.

The two newspapers of the other major newspaper group in Chicago, Field Enterprises, endorsed the same candidates and were more successful than the McCormick-Patterson organization. More than 89 percent of their endorsed candidates won. Did the more successful Field Enterprises group influence the public while the McCormick-Patterson group failed? Or was the Field group simply more in tune with the public's attitudes?

If this problem isn't tantalizing enough, we can always return to the first question, the paradox that Chicago had one of the few political bosses left in America, yet was one of the very few cities that still had competing dailies as well as a plethora of other media.

Atlanta's Cox: No Control

In Atlanta, Georgia, at the time of my survey the nation's 18th-largest communications market, there was considerably less competition, compared to Chicago. The Cox organization owned the only two major dailies in Atlanta, as well as one of the city's major television and radio stations (WSB). Unlike Chicago, which boasted nine local television stations, Atlanta had only five. Cox's media properties reached into every home in the market and faced serious competition from only two of the other four television stations in the city.

In 1968, Cox's television station, WSB, commissioned a study of political attitudes among its viewers. They found that nearly 75 percent of the registered voters in the state watched WSB's programs and that 91 percent of them could identify Hal Suit, the station's newscaster, when they were shown his picture. (Hal Suit subsequently put this public exposure to political advantage by winning the Republican nomination for governor, although he lost to the Democratic candidate in the election.)

Yet despite Cox's formidable position in Atlanta, the following description of the city's mayoral election in 1969 provides a striking illustration of the dubious role of media in directing public opinion.

The longtime and popular Democratic mayor of Atlanta, Ivan Allen, Jr., had retired, and threw his support to his vice mayor, Samuel Massell, a Jew. Massell ran against the Republican alderman, Rodney Cook, a white Protestant. On the Sunday before the election, the Cox media carried news of an alleged shakedown of local nightclub owners by Massell's brother and a detective on the Atlanta police force, for political contributions to support Massell. As a result, Allen shifted his support from Massell to Cook, and even went so far as to request publicly that Massell withdraw from the election. All the while, Cox's newspapers pressed hard for Cook and attacked Massell vigorously. Nevertheless, Massell won overwhelmingly.

The inability of the Cox organization to influence a local election, despite its formidable array of local media, a major issue, the turn-around support of a popular local leader, and a possible religious bias, cannot be attributed to ineptitude. The president of the Cox organization, J. Leonard Reinsch, was the national media consultant to the Democratic Party.

Nor could Massell's success be written off as a Southern knee-jerk reflex favoring Democrats over Republicans. In the gubernatorial elections, Republican candidate Calloway received 425,000 votes to Democrat Maddox's 420,000. (In the absence of a clear majority, the choice was up to the Georgia Legislature, which chose Maddox.)

Notwithstanding the dominant position of the Cox organization in Atlanta, its media were less successful in endorsing eventual winners in local elections than were Field Enterprises' in Chicago, where media competition was more intense. Thus, in 1968, the *Atlanta Journal* was 61-percent successful; the *Atlanta Constitution*, 53-percent. (In 1969, their scores improved to 66 percent and 81 percent, respectively.) It might be noted in passing that the two Cox newspapers did not agree on the endorsement of 30 percent of the local issues and local candidates, though this does not explain their inability to influence the local mayoral election, where both Cox newspapers were in agreement.

Southern Gentility: Meridian, Mississippi

Now let's look at a market that was as nearly sewed up by one media owner as it is possible to be. Meridian, Mississippi, represents the hoariest example of media dominance that could be found among America's 204 markets. The Meridian market as a whole (which covers ten surrounding counties) included 76,300 homes. In population it ranked 151st of 204 markets in the United States (the 204th is the smallest market). Meridian had, in 1970, only one media owner, Mrs. James H. Skewes, whose properties could reach nearly all of the homes in the market. With no real competition, the potential for domination in Meridian was high.

The town's only daily newspaper, the *Meridian Star*, with a circulation of 22,527, was owned by Mrs. Skewes and operated by her son, James B. Skewes. The Skeweses were also sole owners of the market's most widely listened-to AM radio station and had an 11-percent interest in the town's only television station, WTOK, whose shares were widely held. The station carried programs from two networks (CBS and ABC) and was credited by the ARB (the audience rating firm) with 68 percent of the local audience.

Competition from other local media was weak. The next-closest local competitor to the Skewes interests was radio station WOKK, owned by the New South Broadcasting Company, but it reached only 15 percent of the market's homes. There was another television station in Meridian: WHTV, a UHF station broadcasting on Channel 24. It also carried programs from two networks (NBC and ABC), but had a very small share of the market.

As for newspapers, the competition facing the Skeweses' *Meridian Star* came from the *Jackson Clarion-Ledger* and the *Birmingham News* (but both of these papers reached less than 4 percent of the market). Most people in Meridian got most of their news from the Skewes interests. The potential for domination clearly was present. The question is, how did the Skeweses use this potential? Prior to the mayoral primaries and general elections of June 1969, the *Star*'s editorials did not endorse any candidate for any office.

While it was true that Meridian did not yet seem to be the beneficiary of the two-party system, it was still possible that there were some significant issues that could have been raised for debate when a city of 50,000 approached city council elections. But the local media aired none.

In the November 1968 national elections the *Star* did halfheartedly endorse Nixon for president, noting that "Our hearts are with Wallace, but he probably has no chance of winning."

The substantial local business interests of the media stockholders in Meridian may partly have accounted for this reluctance to stimulate local debate. But another explanation lay in the political environment itself. It is reasonably safe to take sides on issues over which people are divided, even if your business depends on their continued public patronage. But it is not so safe when most people are known to hold strong and basically identical views.

In effect, the situation in Meridian illustrated the passive role of local small-town media owners: politically colorless or, at best, adopting the community's outlook. They hardly provided the type of local service envisaged by the FCC when it created a system of local television broadcasters. Often as not, the dominant media owners in small towns do not dominate, they merely plod.

Even though there is no serious competition from media outside the market, it is doubtful that the public in small markets like Meridian would ever be the political captives of the local media owner. In small markets the local political leaders are generally familiar figures to practically every family in the area. There is no need for local political candidates in small communities to rely on television, or any other medium for that matter, in order to obtain exposure to their electorate.

In large metropolitan areas, on the other hand, the situation more nearly resembles the national model, where the public relies on the media for knowledge of its political leaders. Here, however, there are compensating forces at work: In the major markets, where there is in fact greater political reliance on the media, the intense competition among the several dominant media owners (defined as those able to reach nearly every home) is generally sufficient to prevent their dominant position from being translated into real political power. This can be seen in the fact that political bossism in the major markets has been confined to the history books. The substantial strides in the development of mass communications in recent years have not been accompanied by the entrenchment of political power but by an increase in its instability, for reasons we will examine shortly.

Political Advertising

So far, we have discussed the political role of the *owners* of the mass media. But in the United States the ability to use the mass-communications facilities for political purposes is not restricted to its owners. Anyone may "rent" the media to advance the cause of a candidate or an issue through the purchase of newspaper space or air time. This, of course, makes even more suspect the government's great concern regarding media ownership. Indeed, the accessibility of the mass media to those who can afford to pay the price is possibly a more serious social and political issue than is media ownership.

The broadcast media, particularly television, have brought into the political arena an increasing number of people who in the past could not have stood for public office without either winning the support of the old-line party machines or fighting them. Television and radio (and computerized mailings) have enabled them to go directly to the people over the heads of the political machines.

While this has opened politics to fresh talent and introduced a new political style, it also has its problems: It may eventually restrict political activity to the wealthy. Initially, however, it has rendered unstable whatever power had been possessed by local political organizations.

The total cost of political campaigning has leaped. But the broadcast media account for a relatively small and stable part of the cost of political campaigning.

At the national level the greater part of the exposure of presidential candidates on the broadcast media has been obtained *free.* Thus, 85 percent of the network air time used by the presidential candidates was obtained without charge (this was the last such study, 1972).[8] Nevertheless, many hold to the myth that the use of the mass media is responsible for the high cost of political campaigning.

It is also interesting to note that from the standpoint of television, political advertising is a very minor source of revenue. Of the total revenue received for political broadcasting by the three major television networks, most of it has consisted of large blocks of time for political programs such as telethons, film specials, or speeches. The balance has represented receipts from "spot" political advertisements.

All told, only 18 hours of program time are actually purchased from the networks in most presidential campaigns. In addition, and probably more important from the standpoint of its effectiveness, the three networks together provide the candidates with 81 hours of free time on commercially sponsored programs such as *Issues and Answers, Face the Nation*, and the *Today Show*, plus another 21 free hours of nationwide network exposure—a total of 102 free hours, exclusive of network news. Altogether the presidential candidates have free nationwide exposure for the equivalent of more than an hour a day for the 14 weeks between the party conventions and the November elections.[9]

This is a considerable volume of nationwide exposure, and we must keep in mind that the networks are but one part of broadcasting. There are also the local broadcasting stations and of course the regular network news coverage, through which an adroit presidential campaigner can maintain almost continuous contact with the nation without charge.

Actually, political advertising on national (network) television accounts for only 8 percent of the grand total of the funds spent for air time by all political candidates. The rest of the money, or 92 percent, goes directly to the television stations and radio stations, most of it into local "spot" announcements of 60 seconds or less. For the local television broadcasters, political advertising was also a minor item.

In 1972, the large number of free hours shown in Table 8 for radio stations (13,673) represented the donation of time by 5,100 broadcasters. It averaged about 2.6 hours per station. The nation's 700 commercial television stations donated 2,545 hours, an average of about 3.6 hours per station.

Equal Time

Possibly even more free station time and free network time would have been made available in the absence of Regulation 315, which is generally referred to as the "equal time rule." This rule prohibited station licensees from selling paid time or granting free time to one candidate unless an equal amount of time was offered on the same terms to all candidates competing for the same office. Until 1959, this rule also applied to news reports,

Table 8   Free Radio and Television Time Provided for Political
Advertising, 1972 (in hours)

| | TOTAL | STATIONS | | NETWORKS | |
		TELEVISION	RADIO	TELEVISION	RADIO
Primaries	6,899	1,068	5,724	73	34
Elections	9,474	1,477	7,949	29	19
Total	16,373	2,545	13,673	102	53

Source: *FCC Report on Political Broadcasting* (1973).

documentaries, and interviews. It was abandoned in its entirety
in 1987.

In late 1960 the rule was temporarily suspended to facilitate
the Kennedy–Nixon debates, which explains the substantial
number of free hours of nationwide network time donated to
the candidates that year. If the rule had not been suspended,
equal time would have had to be given to all the splinter-party
candidates. The cost, to the networks, of the time donated to the
Kennedy–Nixon debates alone exceeded $2 million.

Some candidates may have wanted to see the rule adhered to,
so that they might avoid a public debate. Certainly, Richard
Nixon probably did not want to have to repeat his 1960 experience. If, however, free time had been provided without
suspending the equal time rule, the 1968 debaters would have
had to include Reverend Hensley of the Universal Party, Eldridge
Cleaver of the Peace and Freedom Party, Dick Gregory of the
New Party, and Bishop Tomlinson of the Theocratic Party. As it
was, these parties had the right to buy air time of the type and du-
ration paid for by the two major parties. Their financial inability
to take advantage of this right effectively foreclosed their ability
to use nationwide television. In 1972, the absence of these splin-
ter parties facilitated the granting of a substantial number of free
hours on national television.

A major shortcoming of nearly all the recommendations regarding political use of the media has been that they focus on the cost of air time on network television, which is a relatively minor cost and one borne only by the presidential candidates. The high cost of campaigning for other government offices or of using the other media has not been considered even by such prestigious groups as the Twentieth Century Fund's commission on campaign costs in the electronic era, whose findings were published in *Voters' Time* (1969). This is an example of the dangers resulting from the mythology surrounding mass communications.

The Future Cost of Campaigning

It is important to note that the rising cost of political campaigning is not entirely attributable to increases in the prices charged by the media. In fact, political ads in the mass media generally receive special discounts. The real problem, as we shall see, is not rising media costs but increased political spending, which in turn is the result of fundamental changes taking place in the structure of political organization in this country.

Elective offices now resemble seats on the stock exchange. There are a relatively static number of elective positions at the state and federal levels and an increasing number of men who have the affluence to compete for them. This necessarily leads to an increase in the competitive cost as candidates try to outbid one another.

In the past, the political party or the local political machine was the gateway to elective office. Today, as already noted, the cost of the campaign is all that stands between an ambitious man of means and the general public. The broadcast media, particularly television, permit him to establish a familiarity in the public mind, a familiarity that has come to replace the party label that guided most voters in past generations. The political clubs are thus rapidly losing their "gatekeeper" function in political life. Then, too, in the past the power of patronage attracted an

army of free local labor to raise funds and ring doorbells for the
club's candidates. But today, how many families will work for a
political candidate in order that a brother or father be rewarded
with a post office job (now no longer a patronage item) or a clerk's
position at city hall?

Another factor to be considered is that today's transient pop-
ulations and suburban outmigration force even the incumbents
to expend considerable effort to make themselves known to their
constituents at primary and election time. The result is an increasing dependence on mass media, media consultants, social
scientists, opinion surveys, mass mailings, and travel.

Furthermore, the films and tapes used in television "spot"
announcements and the research and consultants' fees that
go into them make air time only a small part of the overall
problem. Computerized mailings, billboards, and air travel are
also more significant expenses. These costs have exceeded the
cost of newspaper space and radio and television air time by
200 percent. These are costly replacements for the old system
of patronage and political favors—costs, moreover, that in this
period of weakened political clubs must increasingly be borne by
the candidate on his own.

Congress, whose members are most directly affected by these
changes in the political process, has sought to bring these rising
costs under control. In a very real sense, Congress has sought
to prevent politics from becoming a rich man's game. The result
was the Political Campaign Spending Act (1972). The law applies
to all media and to campaign spending in general. It restricts
campaign expenditures for candidates for federal offices to 10
cents per voter, based on the census estimate for the number
of voters in the area to be represented. Only 6 cents of this
sum, however, may be spent for the use of the mass media. A
minimum total expenditure of $50,000 was allowed under the
new law in cases where the number of voters is fewer than
500,000.

Compared to the actual expenditures of the 1970 senatorial campaigns, the last to be held before it applied, the law was very generous. In only five out of 32 states was more spent in the senatorial campaign than was allowed by law. The five cost overruns in 1970 were not substantial and the majority of the campaigns cost much less than the new legal limit. Thus, in California the 10 cents per voter would allow campaign expenditures of $1,423,000. But in 1970 Tunney (who won) spent only $466,000 and Murphy (who lost) spent only $385,700. In Florida the winner spent $53,900 and the loser $140,000; yet in Florida, the new law allowed expenditures of $508,000, which is almost ten times greater than the sum actually spent by the winner.

Table 9, based on the 1970 senatorial campaign, is of interest in that it not only compares the legal ceiling with actual expenditures, but also shows that in 14 out of 32 contests the winner spent less than the loser. And many of the big spenders were the incumbents. In Massachusetts, Edward Kennedy spent $151,500. His opponent, Spaulding, didn't even try. He spent only $14,900.

The Political Campaign Spending Act was motivated not only by the money issue but also by the fear of the "media men," the fear that with unlimited funds and the consequent ability to hire the best media talent, political know-nothings would populate the landscape. How well founded is this fear?

Confessions of a Media Man

It used to be said that the opponent won because he had a better political machine. Today the popular notion is that the winning candidate's media man was more effective in manipulating the techniques of mass communications, implying that the winner was better at conning the electorate.

A case study of the 1970 gubernatorial election in Michigan, as reported by the winning candidate's media man, Professor Walter

Table 9 The 1971 Legal Limits and Actual Senatorial Campaign Spending, 1970

STATE	CEILING*	DEMOCRAT	SPENT	REPUBLICAN	SPENT
Alaska	$ 60,000	Kay	$ 34,000	Stevens[†]	$ 17,000
Arizona	123,000	Grossman	85,400	Fannin[†]	84,800
California	1,423,000	Tunney[†]	466,700	Murphy	385,000
Connecticut	211,000	Duffey	87,000	Weicker[†]	81,400
				Dodd	49,600
Delaware	60,000	Zimmerman	12,300	Roth[†]	13,600
Florida	518,000	Chiles[†]	53,900	Cramer	140,500
Hawaii	60,000	Heftel	64,900	Fong[†]	27,100
Illinois	756,000	Stevenson[†]	254,900	Smith	235,900
Indiana	350,000	Hartke[†]	182,700	Roudebush	353,000
Maine	66,000	Muskie[†]	30,800	Bishop	8,500
Maryland	271,000	Tydings	92,600	Beall[†]	115,900
Massachusetts	400,000	Kennedy[†]	151,500	Spaulding	14,900
Michigan	597,000	Hart[†]	140,500	Romney	45,000
Minnesota	252,000	Humphrey[†]	158,000	McGregor	166,900
Missouri	322,000	Symington[†]	192,200	Danforth	231,500
Montana	60,000	Mansfield[†]	10,600	Wallace	10,200
Nebraska	100,000	Morrison	21,600	Hruska[†]	26,500
Nevada	60,000	Cannon[†]	68,100	Raggio	73,800
		Williams[†]	179,900	Gross	301,500
New Mexico	63,000	Montoya[†]	35,500	Carter	27,600
New York	1,271,000	Ottinger	648,500	Goodell	570,400
				Buckley[†]	522,400
North Dakota	60,000	Burdick[†]	44,800	Kleppe	71,500
Ohio	716,000	Metzenbaum	238,500	Taft[†]	220,500
Pennsylvania	812,000	Sesler	25,000	Scott[†]	286,600
Rhode Island	67,000	Pastore[†]	16,400	McLaughlin	3,300
Tennessee	271,000	Gore	145,600	Brock[†]	173,400
Texas	760,000	Bentsen[†]	174,700	Bush	292,700
Utah	67,000	Moss[†]	115,300	Burton	91,400
Vermont	60,000	Hoff	69,700	Prouty[†]	53,600
Virginia	320,000	Rawlings	26,200	Garland	31,400
				Byrd[†]	91,900
West Virginia	117,000	Byrd[†]	8,100	Dodson	1,900
Wisconsin	295,000	Proxmire[†]	41,100	Erikson	14,400
Wyoming	600,000	McGee[†]	47,600	Wold	38,700

*Sixty percent of the ceiling may be spent on mass media.
[†]The winning candidate.
Source: *Broadcasting*, May 17, 1971; *Senate Report* (S382), 1971, p. 75.

DeVries, sheds some light on the media man's thinking. DeVries, in a lecture at the Conference on Strategies in the New Politics held at the University of Maryland, described his methodology as being based on two-way communication with the electorate.

First, he showed statistically that his client, Governor William Milliken, should *not* have won the election. In other statewide contests in that election the Republican vote was only 40 percent. Furthermore, his client supported two of three amendments to the state constitution, each of which lost 60–40, and he opposed the third which carried 60–40. Nevertheless, Governor Milliken received 50.7 percent of the vote. How was this managed?

DeVries first sought to establish communication with the electorate by constant polling. It was found that in the last three weeks of the campaign the public's concern shifted from social issues to economic issues. Had constant polling not been employed, this would not have been acknowledged in the campaign and might well have cost them the election.

With a thumb on the public's pulse, the method of responding to its polled attitudes was through news channels. As the incumbent, Milliken had an advantage in this regard, which he exploited. DeVries felt that television was the more important news medium. Thus, the governor had his own cameraman covering his campaign. Almost daily, clips of 30 to 60 seconds were sent to 14 television stations throughout the state. These clips looked like news film and had some news content. Outside of Detroit, Milliken received better than 60-percent coverage. A similar technique was used for radio. In this way the candidate tapped the credibility associated with news and obtained free air time.

To further the newsmaking technique, the governor used press conferences rather than appearances before large audiences. At these conferences he employed audiovisual materials such as slides, charts, and statistical tables, which also made news. His television commercials were similarly designed as miniature documentaries, and focused on a few issues. They were designed to give the impression of personal competence rather than the promise of panaceas.

DeVries's candidate abandoned principle for the public will. He claims that the

> ideal (perfect) way to campaign (or govern) is to have a near flawless, up-to-date, two-way communications system between the candidate and the voters and the capability to respond to the information inputs. . . .   There is nothing Machiavellian about asking what problems bother people, or asking what they think ought to be done about these problems.   Once I find that out, I don't think it Machiavellian to find the best media to inform people what the candidate intends to do or not do about those problems. . . . In short, campaigning (and governing) is an information and communications system.

Something new is clearly evolving to replace the party label, but is it an improvement? The new approach seems to be based in large part on opinion polls. If this approach is used only for campaign purposes, "to tell them what they want to hear," how will the public be able to judge what the candidate will do in office? Instead of giving them his views, it is as if he looked over their shoulders and fed back to them their own.

This new type of candidate may be a sincere technocrat seeking to implement the public will, but then, too, he may be an irresponsible opportunist without a political party's concern for continuity to act as a secondary control once he is in office. These problems are not likely to be solved before they are first laid out on the table and their parts properly identified—least of all, if television is attributed with mystical qualities.

What we are today faced with is an integrated process that incorporates a number of techniques and technologies that have been around a while. Their integrated use is now being put to political advantage by all candidates. No one ignores them. The question is not whether one candidate's media man will find the magic formula before the other candidate's media man.

Rather, the question is whether the process of so-called two-way communication doesn't contain within it a fundamental flaw.

On the other hand, there is much to be said for the concept of maintaining a two-way stream of information between the governing and the governed. Events, issues, and attitudes do change more rapidly today as the public receives information of greater variety and volume than in the past. Pragmatism is a strong tradition in American political life, and the new politics seems to be elevating it to the level of a principle.

Most important, however, in the process described above is the views of the political candidate that are being molded by the public *and not the reverse*. Those who have engaged in political activity have always known this fact of life. Thus, the zest with which the politicians and bureaucrats approach the task of protecting the public interest in communications conceals their more fundamental motivation: concern for the effect of the media on those in the public limelight—on themselves. It was not long before the opinion poll moved out of its infancy as a tool for elections and became a tool for governing.

6 The Government and the Media

Congressional Fear of the Tube

The federal government regulates railroads, trucks, airlines, natural gas, electric power, and the banks, but the politicians and bureaucrats are most concerned about the mass media, particularly television. More testimony, press releases, and threats to our constitutional rights followed from an otherwise not-so-impressive February 1971 CBS program, *The Selling of the Pentagon*, than from a power breakdown that blacked out the entire Northeast, the bankruptcy of the Penn Central Railroad, soaring interest rates, or the worst plane crash. The reason for this is fairly apparent. The politician and the bureaucrat fear any exposure, however benign, that in any way examines the premises and processes underlying public policy. *The Selling of the Pentagon* simply described how the Department of Defense spent taxpayers' money to promote its own view of foreign policy—something most informed persons knew was being done, although it was improper.

The FCC investigated the complaints of some congressmen filed against CBS for its *Pentagon* program and found no basis for citing the network for violation of the Communications Act.

But Representative Harley Orrin Staggers, who was then the Chairman of the Subcommittee on Communications, would not let go. He pressed CBS to disclose its outtakes from the *Pentagon* program, for reasons discussed in the next chapter. When CBS refused, his subcommittee cited the network and its officers for contempt of Congress. The House of Representatives as a whole voted against such a citation. As one journalist posed the issue: Suppose *The Selling of the Pentagon* had been a newspaper article? It would probably have generated an irate letter to the editor, but not much more. And if issue were taken with a newspaper article, it would go through the courts, as was the case in the printing of the Pentagon's Vietnam papers by the *New York Times* and *Washington Post*.

By keeping close tabs on the FCC, which is the licensing authority, Congress maintains a more credible threat to the broadcasting industry (especially television, which is feared the most) than if it kept the FCC at arm's length as it does the other regulatory agencies. For this reason, the trade press and Washington attorneys representing broadcasters earn handsome incomes by keeping a sharp eye on the FCC-Congressional symbioses in order to guide and inform the industry regarding the forces at work in the politically sensitive field of mass communications.

A study of the behavior of Congress and its relationship to the FCC by E. G. Krasnow and L. D. Longley concluded that although major laws affecting the communications industry are rarely enacted, Congress nonetheless exerts a very significant influence on the regulatory agency and on the industry by means of investigations, public hearings, executive sessions, committee reports, and "requests for information."[1]

During a congressional hearing of the FCC, committee members have an opportunity to communicate their views to a captive audience of FCC commissioners, who usually try to portray themselves as flexible, hard-working members of a public-spirited agency. In addition, informal oversight activities take place before and after such hearings.

The FCC commissioners and staff spend much of their time attempting to perceive and anticipate the attitudes of key congressmen and committees. This process, which has been referred to by political scientists as "anticipated reaction," "feedback," or "strategic sensitivity," is an important element in the exercise of congressional authority over the FCC. Alfred Sikes, the FCC chairman appointed in 1989, campaigned for John Dansforth, ranking Republican on the Commerce Committee. His ties to Congress are obvious, in the tradition of the FCC. More recently, however, the FCC has taken second place to a new—and more powerful—force on the media scene: the executive branch.

Presidential Communication

Presidents Nixon, Ford, and Carter did not know how to handle the mass media. They were intimidated by them. It was President Reagan in the 1980s who, as we shall see, was the first to master the art of communicating with the public through ongoing public opinion polls. This permitted him to stay on top of the situation, to know when he was treading on soft ground and when he had the nation on his side. But his predecessors took a different approach. They attacked the media, head-on, often with disastrous results.

Those who preceded Reagan in office tried to outshout the media by taking their case directly to the people. They used the traditional methods of speeches and press conferences. They preempted prime-time programs, and even in lower-keyed activities the president was certain to make the evening news. But this technique began to lose its effectiveness during the Nixon Administration as the networks began to follow up presidential addresses with a critical analysis of what he said. It was inevitable that the two should come into conflict.

The executive branch embarked on its war with the media first by employing the vice president to denounce specific communications companies by name. This was designed to activate the "license syndrome": the fear among broadcasters and networks that they might face unusual problems at license-renewal time. It has been known to be effective.

The president then employed the Executive Office of Communications, which handles press releases, to make an end run around the media to the small-town newspaper, *there* to make their case, which they felt was being distorted by the big media organizations. Unlike Reagan, those who preceded him were in constant conflict with the communications community. Reagan smiled his way past them, knowing which knobs to turn and when. He was secure in the knowledge that he was in tune with the public's mind.

Former President Ronald Reagan was justifiably called the "great communicator." Reagan's secret of how to succeed where others had failed leaked out after he had left office. He gets credit for employing with great success a tool that had been around for a number of years. It was Reagan who first brought polling into intimate involvement in the process of actually governing. Through polling he was able to survive the Iran scandal, which was no less serious a violation of the law than the Watergate break-in that forced President Nixon to undergo the extraordinary step of resigning from office.

President Reagan maintained a public opinion monitoring program of unprecedented scope. More than 500,000 Americans in more than 500 surveys fed him and his advisers intimate knowledge of the public's opinions about world and national events, as well as about the personalities that made these events. These surveys probed just about every aspect of public affairs, on a scale unmatched in American history. Most important and most innovative, these surveys became an integral part of the president's decision making. These polls were far more detailed and exhaustive than any conducted by the media or professional polling companies.

The White House surveys were conducted on a monthly schedule. Each survey was based on an average of 1,500 interviews. Respondents were classified by numerous demographic and socio-economic characteristics. In addition, the White House activated special surveys to study public reaction to extraordinary events such as the bombing of Libya, summit meetings with Gorbachev, and the crash of the spacecraft *Challenger*. There were about 17 such special surveys ordered by the White House, and each involved 800 interviews every two days for a period of several days, with overnight reports to the White House.

Information resulting from many of these studies was defined by state and congressional district for use by White House operatives in order to convince members of Congress to vote for legislation sponsored by the White House. President Reagan's administration knew more about the support or lack of support it had at the grass-roots level than did the Congress, the media, and even local officials. With this knowledge the president could treat with equanimity attacks by the Washington press corps on himself and his policies. These surveys and the information they provided help to explain Reagan's unflappability in the face of circumstances that would have floored those who preceded him into office. The political opinion poll had come of age.[2]

Let's Get 'Em

The Office of Telecommunications Policy (OTP) appeared in the Nixon Administration. For a small office with ill-defined objectives, it had a rather big budget of close to $3 million a year, plus several million dollars of Commerce Department funds appropriated for its Telecommunications Policy Division.

Established in 1970, the tasks of the OTP were vaguely defined. In its first two years, practically every interview with its director,

Clay T. Whitehead, included a question regarding his duties. By 1973, however, he began to define its purposes in a way that can only be described as the development of a mini-FCC, or the President's FCC, as contrasted with the congressional FCC discussed earlier. Early in 1973 the OTP launched a major campaign against the three television networks.

Instead of employing criticism of the type delivered by Vice President Agnew a year or two earlier, the OTP prepared the communications industry for radical surgery. The plan was to separate the broadcasters from the networks and use the former as a control over the latter.

To win over the broadcasting affiliates of the networks, Whitehead proposed legislation (in the name of the White House) that would ease the concerns of television station owners at license-renewal time. He proposed lengthening the term of the license from three years to five. Regarding challenges to renewing the license, the FCC would be required to find that an incumbent's record did not merit renewal before it could designate the renewal for a hearing. The proposed law would also bar the FCC from restructuring the industry on a case-by-case basis (which is how Boston's WHDH lost its license).

But the White House also named its price for this legislation that broadcasters had long desired. Whitehead called upon the broadcasters to exercise "control" over the news coming from the television networks. And, as pointed out by Leonard Zeidenberg in an article in *Broadcasting* magazine, Whitehead let the industry know, in no uncertain terms, that it would punish those whom it felt did not treat news "objectively." As Whitehead put it: "Station managers and network officials who fail to act to correct imbalance or consistent bias from the networks—or who acquiesce by silence—can only be considered willing participants, to be held fully accountable by the broadcaster's community at license renewal time."[3]

To put life into this threat, at about this time local conservatives in Florida challenged the renewal of the licenses of two

Post–Newsweek television stations.[4] Rumor had it that some of the Florida groups were encouraged by, if not actually operating on, the advice of the White House.

Interestingly, it was the staff of the Jacksonville, Florida, station, owned by the Post–Newsweek organization, that brought to light facts that led the Senate to reject the president's nominee to the Supreme Court. Equally significant, it was the subsequent investigative efforts of two *Washington Post* staffers that created a national issue out of the Watergate affair.

Patrick Buchanan, who edited a daily digest of press and broadcast news stories for President Nixon every morning, indicated in an interview for a *New York Times Magazine* article why the White House staff was especially concerned about television: "In terms of *power over the American people*, you can't compare newspapers to those pictures on television. They can make or break a politician. It's all over if you get chopped up on the networks. You can never recover."[5] Again the fear of the power of the media to *manipulate* its audience was motivating public policy, despite the fact that Richard Nixon himself survived such a "chopping up" to become President of the United States.

Attack by the Judiciary

At about the same time that the executive branch began to move aggressively against the mass media, the judicial branch sent a bolt through the industry in the now-famous Caldwell decision, which denied a *New York Times* reporter, Earl Caldwell, immunity from revealing his sources of information when subpoenaed by a federal court.

Within weeks of the Caldwell decision, there followed a number of attempts to get newsmen to identify confidential news sources. Several went to jail. Reporters were also arrested and convicted for receiving and printing the contents of government documents obtained without authorization. In some instances, judges ordered the press to refrain from making public certain information in connection with criminal trials, so as not to influence the jury. The barred information, however, included a jury verdict, the names of witnesses, testimony in open court, and the criminal records of defendants.

So, with its reliability as a source of information long since compromised by misuse of the "secret" stamp and the dissemination of false information, the government now sought to constrain the mass media from probing for the truth. With reporters no longer immune from subpoena, reliable informants would be reluctant to pass information on to them.

Dissenters, in and out of the establishment, no longer have the means of bringing otherwise secret events, plans, and policies to the public's view. This includes disgruntled military men, diplomats, police, Black Panthers, Wall Street executives, and drug pushers. We will never know what this loss of confidentiality will cost, because we will never know what we might have known.

Public affairs are gradually becoming the exclusive preserve of the bureaucracy and of a small group of temporarily appointed and elected officials. Even the current attempt by Congress to write a law that will return to the media some modicum of immunity from subpoena is itself a loss of freedom. By defining the limits of freedom of the press, Congress is now in a position to limit it. A major American tradition has been violated by each of the three branches of the government.

Surprises

As we have seen, the operation of the nation's mass communications system, television in particular, is surrounded by a wide array of pressure groups. These include the FCC, Congress, the president, the Justice Department, the Pentagon, savvy attorneys, public interest groups, the networks, broadcasters, and cable television industry (along with their respective trade associations), and individual large corporations. It is not surprising that all these cooks lead to generally dull fare. Indeed it is a wonder,

with all this overseeing and contesting that television manages
to produce a number of fairly spicy dishes each year. By contrast, the printed media, which are wholly unregulated and almost
untouchable in this regard, are, as a consequence, much more
consistently controversial and exciting in their content. Nevertheless, they cause much less of a furor. The explanation is that
whatever a single newspaper, magazine, or book may report, unless it is picked up and broadcasted by the television networks,
it reaches too few people to be a political threat. In large part,
this protects the printed media from government interference as
much as does the First Amendment.

The way in which the anti-trust laws are applied to the different
media reflects differences in the "power" attributed to these
media. Thus Congress has given special permission for the
joint operation of competing newspapers in half of the 43 cities
where some competition still remains. This policy was made
part of congressional legislation with the passage of the Failing
Newspaper Act of 1970. In addition, tax regulations permitted
the accumulation of undistributed earnings free of the usual tax
of 38 percent for amounts over $120,000, *if the accumulation
was for buying another property of the same type.* This tax
policy encouraged the growth of newspaper chains that today
encompass most of America's major cities, although the number
of newspapers in a chain is not as significant a the size of the cities
they serve. Thus, Tribune's seven newspapers have a combined
circulation of 2.6 million, while Freedom's 20 newspapers have a
combined circulation of only 400,000.

In the broadcasting field, on the other hand, for years the FCC
limited radio and television groups to just seven stations in each
medium, and only in 1985 increased the number to 12.

In general, the government's official treatment of the different
types of media differs, based on their perceived influence. In all
probability, if television stations were not functioning as conduits
for nationwide networks, but were programmed independently
in each market, as was originally intended by the FCC, they

would be less feared by the government. However, the forces of the marketplace have circumvented government policy. There were for a number of years only three "chains" in television, the three networks, though these networks are formed by business contracts rather than ownership. It doesn't really matter who owns the broadcasting stations affiliated with a network since they all carry almost the same programming. The limitation on the number of broadcast stations that can be owned by a single company was therefore not very meaningful. Nevertheless, when the rules were first established, the government evidently failed to anticipate the industry's pattern of development. When this pattern became evident, the regulations were not changed because, as we shall see, government regulation tends to favor the status quo.

The Plan

Given the love-hate relationship between the politician/bureaucrat and the mass media, particularly television, one would not expect public policy in this field to proceed in a rational fashion. One's expectations are not disappointed.

With nearly every American community served by at least one newspaper and several radio stations, the FCC nevertheless chose to create a television system that was designed to provide more local service. As a result, for many years most American communities had fewer than three television stations—that is, three programs—to choose from. Approximately 20 percent of the homes in the United States (48 million people) could not receive more than two television stations. The size of many of the television markets designed by the FCC was simply too small to support more television broadcasting stations. This, of course, led to the growth of cable-TV.

Had the FCC created a system of large regional television markets, each with a substantial number of broadcasting stations, the public would have had at its disposal a greater variety of program choices. In all likelihood, cable television would not have evolved. To some extent, the major markets were regional in character. They were started before the FCC plan was developed. In the major cities, such as New York, Los Angeles, and Chicago, television stations established before 1949 were "grandfathered" into the system. In New York City, for example, stacked up on top of the Empire State Building, are the transmitting antennas of seven different television broadcasting stations, including one that is officially assigned to New Jersey.

If the FCC's plan had been applied to New York City, it is likely that Manhattan, Brooklyn, Queens, the Bronx, and Staten Island would each have their own television stations. But the number of commercial stations available to the residents of each borough would have been fewer than the seven now available throughout the city. The reason is both economic and physical. In economic terms, the fewer the number of homes in the station's coverage area, the fewer the number of stations that can be supported, since the size of the audience determines the amount of advertising revenue flowing into each market. In physical terms, television stations broadcasting on the same or adjoining frequencies require considerable separation, one from the other, to prevent interference. This tends to limit the number that can be located in close proximity.

Most of the television stations on the air in New York City today cover much more than just the city itself. They are regional in scope. Thus, station WCBS-TV, which began operating in 1941, well before the FCC's allocation plan was even conceived, provides television service as far north as New Haven, Connecticut, as far south as Trenton, New Jersey, and westward into Allentown, Pennsylvania. The New York City television market is a regional market.

But in some states investors were caught unprepared. There were no television licenses granted for New Jersey or Delaware before the plan went into effect. There was for many years, only one commercial television station on the air in New Jersey, and Delaware had none at all. In both states, the majority of the viewers relied on television stations in Philadelphia and New York for their programs. The close proximity of the population centers of New Jersey and Delaware to the powerful transmitters in Philadelphia and New York prevented the assignment of spectrum space in these neighboring communities.

Local Service: Seed of Future Problems

For nearly two decades, *local service* was the touchstone of government policy in the field of mass communications. Everything else was secondary. Indeed, the original FCC plan eventually led to the demise (in 1955) of the DuMont Television Network, because there weren't enough markets of significant size to support a fourth network. Had it survived, there would have been four sources of programming instead of the three (ABC, CBS, NBC) that there were until Fox built the fourth network from the large number of independent stations that were licensed in the 1980s.

The FCC felt that local television stations in as many communities as possible would facilitate access to television by candidates for local political office. If a television station's signal covered too many communities, the mayor of one town would bore the viewers in neighboring towns, who, understandably, would have no interest in another community's politics. This underlying objective, however, was basically unsound.

The impossibility of providing at least one television station in each political jurisdiction, or even in *most* political jurisdictions, is evident from a cursory glance at the figures. There are approximately 17,000 towns; 18,000 municipalities; and 3,000 counties in the United States. The FCC's engineers could squeeze out, at most, only about 1,800 channel assignments from the spectrum space set aside for television.

Because so few channel assignments had to be spread as thinly as possible over a great many jurisdictions, many viewers were unable to receive all three networks off the air. The uneven geographic distribution of television stations, already described, was merely the surface effect of the commission's allocation plan. Underneath the surface, it had an effect upon communications policy that has yet to work itself out. As shown below, the FCC's original allocation plan for television eventually led to the extension of federal authority into intrastate communications, and even into the regulation of the manufacture of television sets.

The UHF Problem

Even though the available spectrum space allowed for only about 1,800 television stations to service over 38,000 major local jurisdictions, investors weren't interested in most of them. In fact, by 1973 only about 680 commercial television stations were on the air. By 1988, 1,053 commercial stations and 335 educational stations were active. About 500 are still available. The problem was that nearly 1,000 of the available station licenses were for UHF (Ultra High Frequency) channels 14 through 83, located on the second dial on the television set. (Channels 2 through 13 are in the VHF—Very High Frequency—band.) UHF channels present serious problems for their investors.

To some extent, the UHF problem had its origins in the four-year "freeze" (1949–52) when the FCC did not license new television broadcast stations while it awaited completion by its engineers of the television allocation plan. However, all of the stations licensed before 1949 (a total of 107) broadcast on the VHF band (channels 2 through 13). Thus, during the "freeze" 20 million television receivers were sold, none of which could receive UHF signals. This created a national market composed exclusively of VHF receivers.

After the freeze on new television licenses, the FCC quickly ran out of VHF assignments. Of the approximately 120 UHF licensees who took the chance that UHF would catch on, one-quarter went off the air within 24 months because they had no audience. Forty-four had failed. The capital losses were substantial.

In subsequent years another dimension was added to the UHF problem. VHF television stations, being there first, were the vehicle that brought the three television networks into every major city in the nation. Most UHF broadcasters thus had to obtain their own programs, since the networks were booked up. This means that despite poor advertising revenues due to the small markets (in other words, small audiences), most UHF broadcasters had to pay for all their own programs. By contrast, stations affiliated with a network were paid by the network to carry the network's programs.

There are also technical disadvantages to broadcasting on channels 14 through 83. UHF stations are more expensive to build than VHF stations, and the viewers have great difficulty tuning in to UHF stations. It is difficult to find the UHF station on the second dial and, when a viewer is successful, the picture is generally poor and the sound and color are unstable.

The system of small-town UHF stations conceived by government planners did not take shape, lacking as it did an audience of sufficient size to support either local unaffiliated broadcast stations or, until recently, a fourth network that might provide the economic support not otherwise available.

Ironically, of the small, local broadcasters that are on the air, most are *not* providing local programming. Local programs—such as meetings of the town council, local garden shows, or high school basketball games—do not generally attract large audiences and therefore do not attract much advertising support. Television stations located in relatively small markets lack the financial resources necessary to contribute station time for such programs. Only broadcasters in the large urban markets can and do provide some local service of the type envisaged by the FCC; that is, something other than just local news and weather, and in time periods that attract audiences.

The importance of the UHF problem cannot be exaggerated. In 1972, of 164 commercial UHF stations on the air, 92 (56 percent) were losing money, and 75 of them each lost over $50,000 that year. This problem has persisted into the 1980s.

Solving the UHF Problem, or: How the Other Dial Got There

Still hopeful of creating a system based on "local service," the FCC sought ways to encourage investment in UHF broadcasting stations. To increase the size of the UHF audience the commission asked and received from Congress the All-Channel Bill, which banned from interstate commerce, after April 1964, all television sets that do not have an 82 channel capacity (of which 70 channels are in the UHF band). Thus, through the gradual replacement of existing television receivers, it would eventually be possible for all homes at least to receive UHF signals.

But this policy, like the original FCC plan it hoped to make effective, was not based on an economic analysis of the factors involved, such as the inherent unattractiveness of small television markets, where most UHF assignments are located. Investors are not going to be enticed into setting up UHF television stations simply because UHF receivers are in every home. It is also important that the number of homes in a station's broadcast area be large enough to make the investment worthwhile.

Paradoxically, only in the large markets, with their immense audiences, some numbering in the millions, does investment in UHF broadcasting stations prove attractive. This, however, does not advance the cause of local service. The big cities are already very well served by substantial numbers of television stations. But having applied the weight of government authority to the development of UHF, at considerable expense to the consumer, the FCC now must push and protect UHF development as vigorously as it first championed local service.

Each television set costs more because of its UHF receiver components. Thus, the 70 million sets sold between 1965 and 1970 cost the public a total of about $1.2 billion more than they would have, had there been no UHF. Special UHF antennas cost the public even more.

Thus, the FCC wandered from its original objective of local service into new areas of regulation unrelated to its original goal. Indeed, as described below, the FCC has ceased to champion local service through small markets, although they were originally supposed to have been the beneficiaries of the All-Channel Bill, and is now pushing UHF development—at the expense of television broadcasters in small markets. The FCC encouraged investment in UHF broadcasting stations in the major cities in order to provide some benefits in return for the high cost of requiring UHF reception on all television sets. This goal replaced local service as the driving force behind public policy in the field of television communications in the 1970s. The means became the end.

Enter Cable Television

The FCC's desire for a system of small-town television broadcasters ran into conflict with the public's desire to receive all three network signals. As a result, auxiliary services supported by the public evolved. These included translators and boosters—relatively inexpensive devices that relay a television station's signal beyond its normal coverage area. The devices were used illegally by many communities for a number of years in order to bring in distant signals. Finally, in 1960, the FCC accepted them as part of the industry. By that time, there were nearly 1,000 such devices in use, serving as many communities. But this controversy merely set the stage for the CATV (Community Antenna Television) problem.

A CATV system consists of a fairly sophisticated antenna, generally located high on a tower or mountaintop near the community it is designed to serve. The master antenna can pick up distant (as well as local) television signals not otherwise obtained by rooftop antennas. This fairly expensive apparatus is constructed by a locally franchised company, which then sells the signals it picks up to the local townspeople by connecting their television sets to a cable that runs from the giant antenna through the community.[6]

The first CATV was established in 1960. Nearly 30 years later, in 1989, there were 8,000 cable systems serving 49 million homes in large cities as well as in small towns. The reason for cable's growth is attributable to the radical change that cable systems have undergone. Cable is no longer simply an adjunct to off-the-air reception, filling in the gaps in the government's allocation plan. It is today a source of additional entertainment not available over the airwaves.

As more independent broadcast stations (i.e., not affiliated with a network) and more public broadcasting stations have gone on the air, there was the ability to sell the cable service as a provider of more choices than those available locally off the air even in large cities. This is its basic service. For an additional fee, subscribers can obtain entertainment and information produced especially for cable. These are provided by cable network companies and are distributed to the cable system via satellite. It has become a form of pay TV.

There are about 60 national networks and 30 regional networks in the business of selling special programming to cable systems.

As the years passed, the newer cable systems have also benefited from improved cable technology that allowed them to provide more than the original 12 channels. Today's newest systems use fiber optics. There are about 600 in this category. They can deliver up to 120 channels with higher-quality color and better UHF reception than earlier systems. Most of today's systems offer between 30 and 53 channels. However, not all of these channels offer programs to the subscriber. And much of that which is available is often redundant. There are special channels offering movies, financial information, news, sports, music, and comedy. New cable networks are constantly being created to fill the growing appetite of cable systems. The problem, however, is that it all costs money. The subscribers' pocketbook is as much a limiting factor as is technological capacity.

In the early days of cable's development, the government wasn't keen on the market creating an unregulated means of communication. It believed that the fees collected by cable systems would place them in a position to buy programming that the broadcasters were broadcasting to the public without a direct charge. The FCC staff also feared that in small towns cable systems would distract the already small audiences from viewing the struggling small broadcasters. Despite the fact that not one broadcaster had been forced to close down for this reason, the government insisted that cable systems be regulated. For nearly 15 years—until the deregulation policy of the Reagan Administration—cable systems were tied up with government control.

Cable regulation at the federal level required a radical interpretation of federal authority that was sustained by the Supreme Court. This follows from the fact that cable systems don't cross state boundaries and don't use spectrum space, a national resource. Strictly speaking, cable systems were not the business of the federal government but only of state and local governments—which were also regulating the cable systems.

After following this convoluted evolution of public policy, it may be hard to believe but the FCC abandoned its original objective of protecting the small, local broadcaster. When, in 1966, the FCC issued its rules and regulations for CATV, it revealed that it had all but abandoned the idea of protecting television broadcasters in the small towns from CATV competition. Instead, it forbade the entry of CATV systems only into the top 100 markets. Why? Because the big cities were the only place where investors could realistically be expected to build UHF stations, and the FCC feared that the presence of CATV in the big cities might discourage future UHF investors. Thus, CATV systems were permitted to proliferate in small towns.

In 1972, the FCC altered its objectives again. While making extensive demands on future CATV systems, it relaxed its rules to permit CATV to enter the major markets. In doing so, the FCC now argued that CATV would *aid* in the development of UHF stations (by improving the signals delivered into the home) and that the new, more complex regulations were required to encourage program production. How this would encourage program production was never explained. The essential fact, however, is that bureaucracy and government regulation were expanded. In 1985, with a change in government philosophy, cable television was deregulated.

The Resulting Waste

With a quarter of the nation's available television broadcasting capacity lying idle in the UHF band, a significant part of the spectrum space is being wasted. This is a valuable national resource, for which there is considerable demand from other types of users. Part of this problem is inherent in the nature of television communications. It consumes a large piece of the spectrum. A single television signal occupies enough spectrum space for 1,200 simultaneous telephone conversations, and 82 such channels have been earmarked for television throughout the nation.

A major contender for part of the spectrum space allocated to television is the private two-way radio service. This service is used for communication by police and fire departments; for dispatching maintenance crews in the power, gas, rail, highway, and other utility industries; for the remote control of machinery and industrial processes; for paging of personnel in an industrial establishment; and for doctors or other professionals when they are away from their offices. The expansion of these services would increase efficiency and reduce costs in broad sections of the economy. There is a body of opinion that holds that these services cannot expand effectively in the spectrum space that is presently allocated to them. This problem is reported to be especially acute in large cities, where both private radio services and UHF stations have their greatest potential.

While it helps to reduce the cost of small business, private two-way radio is not itself a small business. Investment in private communication equipment is now a multi-billion-dollar industry.

Pressure for reconsideration of existing spectrum allocation has been mounting. A reallocation of a small part of the spectrum space could provide the private radio services with considerable room for expansion. With this expansion there is likely to occur a decline in equipment costs as a result of production economies, with the result that private two-way radio communication could become a common piece of equipment not only in business, but also in the automobile and in the home.

Errors in Social Engineering

Aside from the distortions resulting from the attempt to impose local service on the television medium, is more local service in fact desirable? Isn't local service more than adequately handled by the radio and newspaper media? As a matter of fact, the degree of localism in news reporting is nowhere as developed as in the United States. Ben H. Bagdikian, in his book *The Information Machines*, points out that in the Soviet Union, metropolitan Moscow has less than 3 percent of that nation's population but its dailies account for 87 percent of all Russian newspaper circulation. The same is true of Japan, where Tokyo-based newspapers account for 70 percent of that nation's newspaper circulation. London dailies also account for 70 percent of that country's newspaper circulation. But the daily circulation of New York City and Washington, D.C., newspapers *combined* accounts for less than 10 percent of the national total.[7]

In effect, there is no real national daily in the United States, with the possible exception of *USA Today* and the *Wall Street Journal*, and each has a circulation of less than 2 million. The American system has always been geared to local news and local advertising. Perhaps too much so. Consequently, when television, an entirely new medium, made its appearance, it should have been employed as a window on the world rather than merely another means of providing local service. The advent of domestic space satellites in 1974 provided an added dimension to this aspect of video communications, but the present system of hundreds of small television broadcasting stations has made this difficult. Ground distribution of satellite signals is made considerably more complex and expensive than it would have been if the nation's television grid had consisted of broad regional markets.

To implement the objective of local service, the FCC did more than just design a highly atomized system. For years it made local service a point of consideration at license-renewal time. Every three years the FCC required that each station draw from its program logs seven randomly selected days of programming from among the three preceding years to constitute a representative week's programming. The second-by-second account of what was broadcast on each of these seven days is sent to Washington. There are 350 to 400 entries in each day, and reports are obtained from thousands of stations (radio and television) for review each year. The result was several million entries. The Renewal Branch of the FCC employs only four people. The task of evaluation is hopelessly lost in minutiae, and the information, even if computerized, is too lacking in meaning to be of any value. The principal objective of these reports, however, is to determine the extent to which the broadcaster was faithful to the government's desire that the broadcaster provide local service.

The FCC had all but abandoned its former requirement of local live programming, and for years had not evaluated much of the data collected in the license-renewal forms. It was just a ritual. The information piled up in Washington.

The concept of local video service was not only poorly conceived, it was subverted by the FCC itself when the commission permitted the evolution of the present television networks. The networks created a coordinated nationwide system of programming that achieved by means of the network affiliation contract what the FCC had opposed in its assignment of spectrum space—a wise oversight.

The experiences of the FCC in the broadcasting field raise serious questions regarding the wisdom of having the government plan the structure of an industry. As will be discussed later, this lesson was not lost on the commissioners when the domestic satellite industry came to them for authorization. The commissioners opened the field to all comers over the strenuous objections of the FCC staff, who preferred a regulated monopoly. One of the first effects of this new policy was a 60-percent drop in AT&T's charges for interconnecting television stations. This is another example of the benefits of the process of creative destruction, discussed earlier, in which even the nation's largest corporation, protected by government regulation, had to bow to the pending entry of new firms and new technology. The industrial planning employed by the government in the field of mass communications was poorly conceived and, in large part, unnecessary.

7 The Professionals

Intelligence: Public and Private

The United States government spends several billion dollars a year and employs tens of thousands of civil servants to gather information from abroad for its own "private" use.[1] This does not include the State Department, whose ambassadors and technical specialists gather information in nearly every country in the world. In contrast to the government's staggering investment in information, the American public relies on not more than 1,400 full-time American correspondents assigned abroad by all the mass media and a supporting staff of about 700 foreign nationals. In effect, the entire nation depends on this relatively small corps of foreign correspondents for knowledge of events abroad and as a check on its own government's activities in matters of foreign policy and national defense.

Although a great deal of the information gathered by the government in no way bears on national security, it is rarely made available to the public. This information, collected at the public's expense, requires the effort of skilled journalists to ferret it out. The power attributed to the media and to journalists is, in fact, lodged not in technology but in the quality and credibility of the information that they may (or may not) provide.

There have been a number of opportunities in recent years by which to evaluate the relative abilities of the public and the private intelligence-gathering systems.

The Bay of Pigs fiasco, the daring raid that failed to find American prisoners in the Sontay prison camp in North Vietnam, the faulty information preparatory to the incursion into Laos, as well as the generally inferior quality of information obtained by the government regarding conditions in Eastern Europe, Southeast Asia, and China, and the failure to accurately assess Soviet and Arab intentions toward Israel in 1973 and to anticipate the creation of OPEC (which raised the price of energy eighteen-fold) give testimony to the poor return on its immense investment in information. By comparison, the general public has been much better served (and at much less cost) by its system of mass communications. This is probably best illustrated by the reporting of the Vietnam War.

In the first half of the 1960s there was little, if any, on-the-spot coverage of Vietnam by the American media. During this period the media merely transmitted to the public the government's press releases. As conduits for government views, the American media helped to paint the administration into a corner with its own rhetoric.

When the American commitment became substantial, the media set up shop in Vietnam. The ABC television and radio network employed, in Vietnam, 30 staffers including correspondents, soundmen, editors, and producers, and spent upwards of $1 million a year on Vietnam coverage. NBC's staff in Vietnam numbered 25 to 30 and it spent about $2 million a year to obtain about 120 hours of regular programs and 15 hours of specials.

The CBS staff in Vietnam numbered about 45 and its costs probably equalled those of NBC. Thus, the three major television and radio networks alone had a staff of over 100 gathering and processing the news there.[2]

In addition to the networks, and the equally substantial commitment of the wire services, there was coverage by individual newspapers and broadcast stations. The cost of sending a correspondent on a month's tour of Vietnam came to about $5,000. In the years following 1967, there were generally about 25 correspondents from American media other than the main network and wire news organizations scouring Vietnam for soldiers from back home for personalized interviews.

Through close-ups of what Vietnam was like on the operational level, including the status of the pacification programs, the treatment of civilians, and the morale of the troops, the public began to understand the nature of this unusual decade of military commitment. The improved coverage of the Vietnam War gave rise to doubts regarding the Defense Department's assumptions, predictions, and general competence. This coverage, however, developed late. An earlier start might have helped to reduce the government's sequence of blunders.

It was not easy going all the way. Correspondents frequently reported that the military lied to them. As a more diplomatic reporter expressed it, he had found people in the U.S. Mission and among the military, who "saw a higher value than the truth." The official news briefings were widely referred to as the "5 O'Clock Follies" since the official information officers conducted themselves as if they were public relations men pushing a product—in this case, the war—and wanted to put it in the best light possible.

Fortunately for all concerned, the military rarely employed outright censorship. Thus, the media eventually helped to correct the nation's and the government's view of reality. This culminated in President Johnson's refusal, or perhaps inability, to stand for renomination for a second term. A poll taken in

1967 by Louis Harris showed that only 18 percent of the public thought that Johnson was "frank and straightforward" regarding the Vietnam War. By comparison, Nixon's credibility factor regarding Vietnam was 43 percent. There probably has never been a more dramatic illustration of the importance of the mass media than its ability to bring to the American people a relatively accurate picture of the situation in Vietnam *despite* the efforts of the American government to the contrary.

By comparison, in France, where the government indirectly controls the media through strict censorship of news sources, people were far less aware of their own government's activities in Vietnam in the 1950s or in Algeria during that equally painful conflict. Indeed, their media did not even inform them of the Paris student riots of 1971. That does not mean that journalists always perform as well as they did in Vietnam. Their coverage of Africa and the Middle East has been grossly inadequate.

The Pentagon Papers

The extraordinary and possibly unprecedented use of subterfuge by President Johnson and his associates may explain the failure of the nation's media to alert the general public and Congress to the nature of the Vietnam affair when it was in its formative stages. The subsequent attitude of the media toward the government is a subject deserving of study in itself, for the media then adopted a skeptical and ultimately hostile attitude, even when it was not warranted. As an example, the media paid little attention to the fact that North Vietnamese troops were in Cambodia and Laos, and instead blamed America for expansion of the war. The media also failed to report the local peoples' hostility to communism. This came to light only later, via the "boat people." But then it was too late.

The turning point of the government versus the media aspect of the Vietnam War was the attempt of the Nixon administration to prevent publication of an historical analysis of America's

Vietnam policy that had fallen into the hands of the media in
April 1971.   The Pentagon's 47-volume history of America's
involvement in Indochina was extraordinary in its revelation of
government ineptitude and fraternal group-think.   There was
none of the exposure of military secrets that the government
alleged would occur. The public and the professional journalist
again found that the government though headed by a new
president and a different political party, was nevertheless intent
on protecting the boys in the backroom from public exposure.

The salutary effect of the controversy over publication of the
Pentagon Papers was the Supreme Court ruling.   In an age
in which the chief executive alone can commit the nation to
costly and often irreversible policies, early public scrutiny of
the assumptions underlying government policies has become an
essential part of the democratic process. This can be assured only
through the free flow of information.

Justice William Brennan noted in his concurring opinion that
"never before has the United States [government] sought to
enjoin a newspaper from publishing information in its possession." Justice Potter Stewart took particular exception to the
government's desire to protect itself by classifying its documents.
"When everything is classified, then nothing is classified." Justice
Hugo Black expressed the opinion that

> the press was to serve the governed not the governors.   The
> government's power to censor the press was abolished so that the
> press would remain forever free to censure the government. . . .
> Paramount among the responsibilities of a free press is the duty to
> prevent any part of the government from deceiving the people.

Public knowledge of the number of troops committed to Vietnam (over 500,000); the number of men killed (over 45,000)
and wounded (over 250,000); the large number of aircraft lost
(over 6,000); the generally high economic price ($2 billion a
month); the lack of control over the Vietnamese countryside despite the vast commitment reported by the media; the awareness

of government deception; and the moral issues raised by the war (especially its effect on the people we were supposedly defending) all led to the public's rejection of the government's Vietnam policy.

Once the facts started to flow, America's media, rather than its democratically elected government, held the confidence of the people. The effect that this experience will have on the concept of government deserves more attention than it has yet received from scholars, the media, and the government. In time, its implications could be profound, and not only for the American people. It is worth noting, however, that the disclosure of the Pentagon Papers appeared in the press and not on television (as was the case with Watergate, as well). So much for the *power* of modern technology.

Secretiveness

The task of the professional journalist is clear. He functions as the antagonist of the bureaucracy. His objective, if not his duty, is to make public that which the bureaucracy seeks to keep confidential. Rarely is national security at issue. The secretiveness of government employees is for their own protection rather than for the protection of the nation. Foolishness, waste, and the desire to accumulate and wield power for its own sake are some of the motives underlying their secretiveness. As an example, the cloak of executive privilege was extended to the following important questions:

1. The Defense Department refused to produce generals to testify before a congressional committee regarding army surveillance of civilians.
2. The State Department would not discuss its plans or explain its policies as regards foreign economic policy (Congress subsequently voted to discontinue the foreign aid program).

3. The executive branch would not explain to Congress the standards for listing *American* citizens in an internal security computer.

These are examples of information requested by *elected* officials of *appointed* officials which the latter chose to conceal. Yet in startling contrast to the government's secretiveness regarding the domestic and economic policies listed above, the following article appeared in the *New York Times* on October 6, 1971. It was filed by Reuters, a European news service:

FB-111's DEPLOYED WITH NUCLEAR ARMS

Omaha, Oct. 5 (Reuters)—The FB-111 bomber, a descendant of the politically controversial and trouble-plagued TFX, has begun to take over some of the burdens of the United States nuclear deterrent force, the Strategic Air Command disclosed today.

At least 12 of the swing-wing planes are now on constant ground alert at SAC bases in the Northeast.

Each of the supersonic planes is armed with six nuclear bombs with a total yield of about five megatons, equal to the explosive force of five million tons of TNT.

Four of the weapons are nestled in bomb bays and one is mounted on an external rack under each wing.

The bombers are poised on alert pads at Pease Air Force Base at Portsmouth, N.H., and at Plattsburgh Air Force Base in northern New York.

The command acknowledged today that a portion of the FB-111 force had been written into the nation's nuclear war plan, an integrated operations plan for all strategic forces of the United States and the North Atlantic Treaty Organization. But a spokesman at SAC headquarters here said he could not disclose the exact number of FB-111s that had been declared operational.

Isn't this information the "real stuff," the sort that cloak-and-dagger types risk their lives to get their hands on, the sort of information that should be classified? It could be bought for the price of a newspaper.

This brief comparison between what the government reveals and what it conceals illustrates what those who observe the government at close range have always known: that American news reporters and not "foreign powers" are the government's principal adversary. It is from the American journalist, and therefore the American public, that most documents are classified. In this the government acknowledges that the real power of the media is not that they can *influence* the public but rather that they can *inform* the public. The power with which the media are generally credited is inherent in *what* they communicate. It is the facts, not the media, that possess power. To the extent that the bureaucrats can keep the facts that underlie their decisions to themselves, their power is enhanced. Conversely, to the extent that the public is informed, *its* power is enhanced.

The contest over the control of information is a contest over the sum and substance of power. To share information is to share the essence of power. The effect of the journalistic function is thus to temper the government's attempts to make the governed more easily governable. On the other hand, the extent to which the governed are informed of their government's activities is the extent to which their freedom is assured. The conflict of interest is obvious and is inherent in the roles played by the protagonists.

Examples of tension or built-in conflict are many, and they are increasing of late. In this contest for facts, the truth has been sought regarding the administration's policy on a wide range of issues, including ecology, arms sales, consumer protection, energy, and the federal budget.

The Selling of the Pentagon *Affair*

The journalist's power to inform, however, is not beyond corruptibility, noble though his intent may be. If the journalist or the owners or managers of the media themselves tamper with the information obtained from their investigative activities, then their credibility (that is, their "power") is endangered and with it their function as the public's information-gathering service.

Several vital issues once inadvertently combined over a single television program that focused attention on this problem. It involved the CBS television documentary on the Defense Department's domestic public relations activities, referred to in the preceding chapter. The CBS documentary *The Selling of the Pentagon* was broadcast nationwide in the spring of 1971. The program was attacked by the vice president and by several members of Congress on the grounds that it engaged in unusual distortions. It was charged that the program's producer took words uttered by the Pentagon official in answer to one set of questions and used them as answers to a different set of questions.

Representative Harley Staggers of the House Commerce Committee subpoenaed CBS's original film from which the program was assembled to investigate these allegations. Dr. Frank Stanton, the then-president of CBS, refused to produce them on principle, citing the First Amendment on freedom of the press. The committee found him in contempt—a finding that failed to pass a vote of the full House. At which point this highly celebrated affair disappeared from public view. It was, however, a very significant encounter.

The affair was two-sided. The reaction against the program was in truth motivated by its conclusions: that the Defense Department was spending the taxpayers' hard-earned money to propagandize the same American taxpayers to favor increased arms expenditures. This, indeed, was an activity unbecoming this particular agency of the government. In addition, a number of examples of the Defense Department's public relations techniques shown in this documentary were distasteful. These included a demonstration of how to kill an adversary, performed at a shopping center in Ohio before an audience of children and housewives. The documentary also reported on movies shown to the public in which the Defense Department advocated a particular approach to foreign policy—a public relations activity in which even the State Department does not engage.

These were clearly issues of considerable importance, though unsensational since they were no secret to anyone who took an interest in such matters. Staggers's committee did not fault the program's conclusions but sought to impugn them on the grounds that the program's producer engaged in questionable "editing" techniques. On this issue, Staggers was supported by the evidence.

The zealousness of the CBS news team caused their editing to get in the way of their reporting. They did, in fact, so radically alter the sequence of responses in an interview that their critics were able to shift the public's attention from the program's content to the program's techniques and in the process to challenge the medium's credibility.

Thus, in editing their news tapes CBS presented as a direct six-sentence quotation a statement from a colonel composed of a first sentence from page 55 of his prepared text, followed by a second statement from page 36, followed by a third and a fourth from page 48, a fifth from page 73, and a sixth from page 88. When shown on television, it appeared that the colonel's reply was made verbatim as shown.

In the same documentary, a sequence with Daniel Henkin, Assistant Secretary of Defense for Public Affairs, was so manipulated that it affected the meaning of the response. The following is an example of this form of editing. The program, as shown on the air, contained the following question and reply:

> ROGER MUDD (CBS): What about your public displays of military equipment at state fairs and shopping centers? What purpose does that serve?
>
> MR. HENKIN: Well, I think it serves the purpose of informing the public about their armed forces. I believe the American public has the right to request information about the armed forces, to have speakers come before them, to ask questions, and to understand the

need for our armed forces, why we ask for the funds that we do ask for, how we spend these funds, what are we doing about such problems as drugs—and we do have a drug problem in the armed forces—what are we doing about the racial problem, and we do have a racial problem. I think the public has a valid right to ask us those questions.

This, on the other hand, is how Mr. Henkin *actually* answered the question:

> MR. HENKIN: Well, I think it serves the purpose of informing the public about their armed forces. It also has the ancillary benefit, I would hope, of stimulating interest in recruiting as we move or try to move to zero draft calls and increased reliance on volunteers for our armed forces. I think it is very important that the American youth has an opportunity to learn about the armed forces.

The answer Mr. Henkin was *shown* to be giving had been transposed from his answer to another question a couple of pages along in the transcribed interview. In that sequence, Mudd had asked Henkin whether the sort of thing he was now talking about—drug problems and racial problems—was "the sort of information that gets passed at state fairs by sergeants who are standing next to rockets." To which Henkin replied:

> MR. HENKIN: No, I didn't—wouldn't limit that to sergeants standing next to any kind of exhibits. I knew—I thought we were discussing speeches and all.

Here is how the same exchange was edited for network television:

> ROGER MUDD: Well, is that the sort of information about the drug problem you have and racial problem you have and the budget problems you have—is that the sort of information that gets passed out at state fairs by sergeants who are standing next to rockets?
>
> MR. HENKIN: No, I wouldn't limit that to sergeants standing next to any kind of exhibit. Now, there are those who contend that this is propaganda. I do not agree with this.

The part about discussing "speeches and all" had been omitted; the part about propaganda comes from a few lines above Henkin's actual answer and was, in fact, a reference to charges that the Pentagon was using talk of the "increasing Soviet threat" as propaganda to influence the size of the military budget.

In the resulting hullabaloo even the First Amendment privileges were unnecessarily exposed to danger when Representative Staggers subpoenaed the program's original materials. This might have been another precedent for limiting the profession's right to privileged information. Staggers knew all along precisely what changes had been made by CBS in its editing. His committee was simply out to penetrate the veil that protects the journalist's sources and the confidentiality of their work materials.

This affair uncovered an extremely important issue: It highlighted the fact that news reporting and advocacy are inherently incompatible. Excessive zeal on the part of reporters in advancing a point of view violates the profession's function. In effect, "advocacy journalism" is a contradiction of terms. Those who advance this school of thought have abandoned concern for the journalist's credibility in favor of their own point of view. It is an arrogance born of the myth that the media are powerful because the audience is malleable. But the public is not weak-minded, as some believe. Facts are enough to call their attention to the issues.

Opinions and Views

Editorials and news analyses have their place in the media, but they should not be blended with the straight news reporting that is the backbone of mass communications. From the public's standpoint there is no difference between those who advocate a point of view out of sincerity and those who are motivated by monetary or psychological considerations. In the end, the public is shortchanged in the accuracy or comprehensiveness of the information it receives.

The principal international issues raised in the media for a number of years have been events in South Africa and the Palestinians. However, neither of these issues has received a well-rounded presentation. The media have been immersed in journalistic moralizing in place of dry, objective, and comprehensive reporting. The average informed American thinks that the South African issue devolves on just two problems: apartheid and one man, one vote.

We have had no reporting on the inner workings and interrelationships among the many African tribes in South Africa, what their plans are relative to each other as well as toward the "colored" and the whites. Nor do we hear about the African experience elsewhere on the continent, from which conclusions might be drawn as to what may be expected if those we see and hear on television have their way.

The case is similar with Israel and the Palestinians. Few Americans are aware of the size of the "captured territories" that have dominated news from the Middle East. Very few people seem to know that the whole of the "territories" out of which Palestinians would create a country is only 30 miles wide and 70 miles long, not as large as some American farms and ranches. Nor do many realize that the Arabs possessed this land for 19 years and themselves never created a Palestinian state from it. And not many Americans are aware of how it came into Israel's possession. If the facts were known, would Palestinians get the press coverage they are now getting?

One would think that there is nothing to report on elsewhere in Africa and the Middle East. What has happened to the oil wealth in Iraq, Saudi Arabia, and Nigeria? How are blacks and Arabs treating *their* minorities?

Americans have been kept in the dark about the inner turmoil in Northern Ireland, except to hear of it when a bomb goes off. Similar criticism can be directed at the media regarding events among millions of India's Untouchables; the Sikhs in Punjab; the Sri Lankans (where is that, you ask?); the Kurds in Iraq; the Soviet consumer; the massive population transfers in Tibet and in the Balkans. The list is almost endless.

The reason that most of us are poorly informed is that journalists and media people in general have made a cause of selected issues and focus on them almost to the exclusion of all else. We can go to church and synagogue for sermons and lessons on the *meaning* of world events; we turn to journalists and the media for *information*. Dry information. Facts. In recent years the American people have been shortchanged. And, to our great misfortune, so have our leaders, who also rely on the media for much of their information.

Actors or Critics

So great is the activist urge today that many journalists have even gone beyond advocacy and become actual participants in the events—in effect, have themselves become news makers.

The power of the media, however—and this cannot be stated often enough—is based not on its technology but on its credibility. The impropriety of reporters, editors, publishers, or media owners participating in the events on which they report is a serious threat to the role of the media as a reliable source of information in the American system.

There is today considerable confusion regarding the proper role and behavior of the professional journalist, editor, and media owner. Is it a bribe when a member of the news staff, a news editor, a publisher, or a broadcaster accepts gifts, awards, free trips, or tickets to entertainment events? *Editor & Publisher*, a leading trade journal, lists more than 130 prizes for newsmen. The source of many of these "awards" are special-interest groups. They offer prizes ranging up to $2,500. The winner of the Pulitzer Prize, by comparison, receives only $3,000. These sums are relatively small, but then so was the value of the vicuña coat accepted by Sherman Adams, President Eisenhower's powerful executive assistant who was drummed out of office after the media disclosed his acceptance of this "token of appreciation" from an industrialist.[2]

Should those serving the public in the field of mass communications be any less scrupulous? Should they become involved in politics? Should they write speeches for political candidates, manage campaigns, advise candidates on the use of media, and generally hobnob with politicians or representatives of special interests?

Herbert Klein, a former White House Communications Director, alternated between being editor of the *San Diego Union* and political activist for Richard Nixon. (He later became vice president of MetroMedia Corporation.) Erwin Canham, editor-in-chief of the highly respected *Christian Science Monitor*, lobbied for revenue sharing, and served as president of the U.S. Chamber of Commerce. Tom Wicker, a columnist and associate editor of the *New York Times*, has made a number of public appearances in which he attacked American foreign policy. Arnaud de Borchgrave, a senior editor of *Newsweek* assigned to the Middle East, had been active on behalf of Anwar Sadat, President of Egypt.

Can the public rely on the media's objectivity in news reporting when its reporters, editors, publishers, and owners unabashedly compromise themselves financially and politically? Unlike political institutions, whose public trust is inscribed in the statutes, the media now float in an undefined space that separates commerce and its credo, *Caveat emptor*, from the ethically defined professions of law, medicine, and politics.

At some point, and soon, the media professionals—from reporters to owners—will have to decide whether they are participants or observers. To investigate and to report the facts is the duty of the media's professionals. To attempt to lead the public is to take sides, to have a vested interest; in effect, to abandon objectivity for commitment. At that point, the media professional has changed professions: He has become a politician or a propagandist. If this involves an editor or an owner, he has, in effect, converted his medium from a dispassionate and uncommitted source of objective information into a party publication or party broadcast facility. In truth it cannot be played both ways.

A Profile

Who are the professional journalists? What kind of people are they? Is there any substance to the romantic figure drawn by American fiction?

A survey of foreign correspondents published by Leo Bogart in 1968 reported that the typical foreign correspondent is a married male in his forties, a college graduate with over ten years' experience in journalism, and not less than three years in his foreign post. His closest friends include local foreign nationals, whose newspapers he reads regularly and whose language he is able to speak fluently (except generally, for those in Asia).

Nearly half of those responding to Bogart's survey reported that they have considered themselves political "liberals," 38 percent thought of themselves as moderates, and 10 percent as conservatives. Nearly 60 percent identified with the Democratic Party, 21 percent with the Republican, and 15 percent were independents.[3]

The old "front page" image of the young free-lance high school dropout whose style was more swashbuckler than academic, who was more detective than researcher, is a myth. Fewer than 4 percent of all correspondents serving the American media abroad did not attend college. Three-quarters of the foreign correspondents are college graduates; a third of these attended graduate school. About 94 percent of all foreign correspondents are accompanied by their wives and children.

In fact, the foreign correspondent serving the American public is an educated and seasoned professional who is steeped in the

knowledge of the environment to which he is assigned. He is also
well paid.

Domestic Journalism

At home, the nation's capital is the prestige news center. The
resident press corps in Washington numbers approximately 1,250
full-time professionals, nearly the same number serving American mass media abroad. Hopefully, what they produce is a
balanced account of the government's views, relevant facts that
they are able to assemble, and the views of the opposition.
The information sent to their home media by the members of
the Washington press corps, however, is subject to assault by a
veritable army of publicly financed full-time government public
information specialists—at the last count numbering 5,200 in the
executive branch alone.

During the Nixon Administration, the president's Office of
Information had, to some extent, drawn upon this immense
resource to make an end run around the Washington press corps
by sending copies of speeches and press releases directly to local
newspapers and broadcasting stations. President Reagan, as we
have already noted, went one step further. He maintained an
ongoing poll of grass-roots opinion and, in effect, conducted a
dialogue with the public over the heads of the media.

In addition to the press corps, approximately 13 radio and
television broadcast groups have special news bureaus in Washington. The average capital news bureau files between 60 and
100 items a week. None of these news bureaus cover the basic
news events or the White House, since the radio and television networks and the wire services perform this function. The
news bureaus focus on Capitol Hill and provide their local audiences with special angles and coverage of important but less
conspicuous issues of interest to a specific locality.

The Brookings Institution, a highly regarded policy-research
organization located in Washington, D.C., published in 1981 a

special study of journalists who serve America's mass media in the nation's capital. Like Bogart's study a decade earlier, they found that most reporters on this prestigious beat were liberal, college educated, male, white, and middle class. What they enjoyed most about their work was their personal contact with people who are in the news. They generally shunned research. The study found that

> Washington reporters use no documents in preparing nearly three-quarters of their stories. When reporters do use documents, they rely most often on newspaper articles, "verifying" information by referring to what they or their colleagues wrote before. Given that most stories are produced under deadline conditions, there is a high potential for perpetuating error.[4]

Regarding the much-vaunted criticism that newspaper chains represent domination by the few, the Brookings Report found that the bureau for a single newspaper operates under closer editorial control from the home office than do those serving a chain. Chain newspaper editors tend to defer to the expertise of their Washington operation. Stated bluntly by a Washington bureau chief, "They don't give a shit about the news. They're business people. I was told to proceed on the theory that if you don't hear from us you're doing a great job. I never hear from them. They never told me to write or not to write a story in six years."[5]

The report also found that newspaper chains focus most on Washington news that relates to or affects the regions served by their newspapers. Thomson Newspapers, for example, filed 2,829 stories in a single year, of which only 139 were categorized as national news. The chain relied on the wire services for national news. By comparison, only 16 percent of the news filed by independent news bureaus (serving a single newspaper) were of local interest.[6]

Although it might seem a force for standardization, group ownership of newspapers has not had this effect on the news produced by the chain bureaus in Washington. The reason is that they focus more on news of regional interest than do the independents. The Brookings Report states that "some papers that have become part of a chain have Washington reporting about their regions for the first time."[7]

The report also found that Washington reporters "initiate the vast majority of their stories and that the stories get good placement and hardly any editing. . . . The decisions are most often made in the field and not in executive suites. The reporters, collectively, cover what interests them and do not cover what does not interest them."[8]

A very serious problem, however, was highlighted by the report. The fact is that 92 percent of the journalists felt that "pack journalism" was a problem. This means that the issues and the perspective given the issues by the various news bureaus tended to be homogeneous. This may follow, in part, from concern that their reporting on national issues not show significant variations or departures from what was being reported over the wire services, over television, or in the prestigious newspapers such as the *Washington Post* and *New York Times*. This is one of the sources of group-think that characterizes the intellectual community.

It appears that the focus of media literature on the ownership of the media as the source of anti-social conspiracies is rank demagoguery. The evidence clearly points to the foot soldiers of the media—the front-line reporters—as those who bear the principal responsibility for what the American people hear and see.

Pundits

The "stars" of journalism are neither the foreign correspondents nor those assigned to the nation's capital, prestigious as they may be, but rather the columnists and pundits.

The television pundits and star-class anchormen are the highest paid of their profession, and earn considerably more than newspaper columnists. But columnists are generally better paid than news editors. Art Buchwald has been reported to be the nation's highest-paid columnist, with earnings from his column and from lecturing reaching well into the six figures.

Clearly, news columns generate large incomes for their syndicates. Jack Anderson's *Washington Merry-Go-Round* annually grosses about $600,000 for its syndicate. Most successful columns bring in about $400,000 a year. Generally, the syndicators split the column's income 50–50 with the columnists. The columnists, who must pay their own expenses, and have to write three articles a week, have little time for thought or research. The consequence is that they displace newspaper space that might be put to better use, particularly news reporting. The problem, however, is that for the subscribing newspaper syndicated columnists are relatively inexpensive, whereas reportage is expensive (and dangerous).

For example, a small newspaper may pay as little as $30 a week for Buchwald's column, since the syndicate salesman either sells cheap or not at all. The top prices paid for columns in larger cities, where there is some newspaper competition, run as high as $1,500 a week. More typically, in most large cities columns are available for about $500 a week. This is half the lowest weekly salary paid a reporter on the larger dailies.[9]

The economics of the situation clearly indicate that newspaper columnists and television and radio pundits will be an important part of the media scene for some time. Indeed, it is surprising that there are so few, considering the relative costs involved. Unfortunately, few of the columnists and pundits have carried on the tradition of investigative reporting that Drew Pearson made his hallmark. But, as Jack Anderson, his successor, can testify, investigative reporting can be very risky. It is generally safer to be either witty or passionate about current events.

Is the Public Gullible?

We have already noted that those who write about the media more often than not try to direct the attention of the public to the sinister potential resident in the type or number of owners. But with rare exceptions—most of which have been collected and related in the media literature—corporate ownership of media is not sought after for any other reason than to make a profit.

The real, ongoing, day-to-day power that exists in mass communications is in the hands of those who are directly involved in collecting and disseminating information. These are the professional journalists and those who write, direct, and produce the entertainment programs into which are necessarily woven the issues of the day.

The professional, whether working for the printed or the electronic media, does have power. That power is not to influence so much as to mislead. This is not implicit in the technology at his or her disposal, but rather in the quality of the material passed onto the public. Is it complete? Is it balanced? Does it reflect and provide a real understanding of the issue? Or, as the Brookings study showed, is there a serious problem of "running with the pack"?

"Group-think," as George Orwell termed it, is the real threat. Are the journalists and the writers of the situation comedies, family dramas, and talk shows pushing a product, as the advertisers do? Are they all implicitly involved in collusion as to what is noble and what is ignominious, so that the public fails to get a balanced picture? The answer to these questions is, unfortunately: Yes. The uniformity of the information, and the uniformity of the evaluation of the information that one reads, sees and hears is an indictment of those who serve in the system. Try as they may to deflect responsibility onto the corporate managers, the responsibility is clearly that of the professional writers, editors, and directors.

Simply because the public buys the product doesn't necessarily mean that it is satisfied with it.   They have no alternative. From time to time, media owners themselves test the market to see if public is in fact satisfied with the product.   In 1985 the Times Mirror Company began a series of surveys to test American attitudes toward the mass media.   Employing the Gallup organization for this purpose, it found that "there has been a serious erosion of public confidence in the media as an objective reporter of the news and as an impartial observer of the political and social scene. The number of Americans who give most media organizations a low believability rating has risen sharply."[10]

The negatives showed up in the public's attitude toward how the media professionals do their job. The study found that 69 percent of those surveyed thought that the media tended to favor one side (up from 53 percent in 1985). Those believing that reporting was actually inaccurate rose from 34 percent in 1985 to 44 percent in 1989.

When these questions were put to the professionals, i.e., to members of the working press, 68 percent felt that they were fair to all sides of the issues—the reverse of the public's perception almost to a man. Among business leaders on whom the media professionals try to lay the blame for everything, it was found that 92 percent felt that the media were generally one-sided.

As for accuracy, 84 percent of the professional journalists felt that they were accurate, half again as many as among those whom they would inform: the public itself. Business leaders had an even more jaded perception of media accuracy: Only 23 percent felt that the information they were receiving was accurate.   Interestingly, what the survey referred to as the "academic elite" tended to agree with the general public. And half of the general public felt that a requirement that news organizations cover all sides of an issue *ought to be written into the law*. That says a great deal regarding the purported gullibility

of the public. It also says a great deal regarding the mystique of
the purported "power of the media."

8 The Underground

Television Youth

Probably no group in our society is more likely to reflect the influence of television than today's adults. Remember that today's average young adult spent approximately 4,000 hours in front of the video screen even before his first day of school. If television exerts a deep influence on people, their values and behavior should in some way reflect the impact of this tremendous exposure. What, in fact, has been the nature of their experience and their behavior?

One of the more noticeable characteristics of children's programs is that they carry twice the number of commercials as do adult programs (16 per hour). Television thus makes the American child a premature participant in our consumer society. By circumventing the natural barrier of illiteracy among the two-to-six-year age group through the visual appeal of its images, television has succeeded in introducing children very early to products and even brands that would not otherwise come to their attention.

Observers of this phenomenon emphasize the ease with which children's appetites are thus stimulated and at the same time the equal ease with which they have been conditioned to expect their desires to be satisfied. Most mothers are pleased to respond to what seems to them a simple enough preference on the part of the child for an item that would be purchased in any event. A survey of 1,500 mothers undertaken by the ABC Television Network as early as 1967[1] revealed that 65 percent of the mothers take their children with them when they go to the supermarket. In the majority of cases, children influenced the mother in the selection of cereals, soft drinks, snacks, toothpaste, and soups. It was also estimated that, on the average, $1.66 more was spent each week for products specifically requested by children. Based on approximately 18 million households with children, this added up to over $1 billion a year of *additional* spending by parents as a result of their children's influence. Since this survey, inflation has more than likely trebled these figures.

Because of his purported responsiveness to suggestion and his influence at home, the preteen viewer is an important member of the television audience. By the age of two, children are counted in audience ratings. And children between the ages of two and eleven make up nearly 23 percent of the viewing population.[2]

Surprisingly, the younger generation has not matured into a generation of avaricious fiends. Indeed, the very opposite has occurred. The principal characteristic of the first generation of young adults who grew up with television has been their rejection of "materialism" and the lifestyle it engenders. Either their early experience as consumers immunized them to the pleasures of pursuing possessions or television's influence was transitory and more powerful cultural forces were at work.

An unexpected product of their early and intense exposure to the mass media is their extraordinary understanding of mass communications. *En masse*, the youth of this period revealed an astonishing knowledge of the technical and psychological aspects of this complex subject. They knew for example, that to call attention to their ideas—which were in opposition to a broad range of political and social policies and institutions—they would have to antagonize and, at the same time win over, the older generation. Thus, intuitively, without a central plan, America's youth coalesced into an amorphous "movement" and created a counterculture that challenged the superficial customs and mores a society holds more sacred (without fully realizing it) than their gods. At the same time, they created several nationwide news services that linked together a formidable underground newspaper system—with no one planning, directing, financing, or even calling for their creation.

As we shall see, they were successful in almost every one of their objectives, even to the point of winning over the older generation to their countercultural innovations that were intended simply as the irritant to call attention to their social and political program.

A by-product of the youth rebellion of the 1970s has been the lessons that it taught regarding the state of mass communications in the United States. They faced no serious legal or economic barriers in their media enterprises—evidence that there is free entry in this field. More important, considering the views to which their media gave expression, they showed that there is still much to be said for the American reputation for political freedom.

The Movement and Its Media

The growth of the underground press from its inception in 1964 is amazing. In his book *The Underground Press* (Indiana University Press, 1970), Robert J. Glessing listed by name over 450 different underground newspapers published in nearly every city in the United States. He estimated that at their peak they had a combined circulation of about 5 million. When multiple readers of each copy are considered, a total audience of about 10 million was probably a conservative estimate of the "reach" of the underground press. Considering that there were then 20 million high school and college students in the United States, this represented a substantial part of American youth. In addition to newspapers this audience was served by several hundred college radio stations that reached millions of young people on and off campus. Many commercial radio stations also appealed to their taste, as did several magazines.

The devotion of this audience to its media was evident from the fact that these media drew hundreds of thousands of young people from great distances to events ranging from rock music concerts to political demonstrations.

These "underground" media were underground in spirit rather than in response to any real need for secrecy. Therefore, despite the fact that some of the underground newspapers published details on how to make Molotov cocktails, how to make false claims for "lost" travelers checks, how to charge another person's telephone for long-distance calls (in 1970, AT&T reported $22 million worth of "free" calls; in 1965, the total had been less than $3 million), almost no one went to jail. Nearly all of the underground newspapers in the United States were sent through the mail, hawked on street corners, and were available in shops catering to young people and students. There was in fact, not the slightest resemblance between the American "movement" and its "underground" media and the *samizdat* papers circulating at the time in the U.S.S.R.—or between the treatment accorded those involved in these activities here and that in the U.S.S.R.

True, some of these publications were on occasion, harassed by local authorities (sometimes for good reason, as when the now-defunct *Washington Free Press* pictured a local magistrate masturbating with the subtitle "He Comm D'Judge"). Usually this harassment was uncalled for, as when underground papers were indicted for obscenity in cities where "adult bookstores" operated; or when youthful street vendors received tickets for jaywalking when stepping off the curb to sell their newspapers; or when printers were induced not to service them. In New Orleans, harassment had gone to such lengths that one underground publication won a federal restraining order enjoining the city and state police from harassing the newspaper's vendors. The overall effect of this harassment, however, had not been repressive. The publications increased in number and in circulation. They ceased publication when the editors or their readers lost interest.

The "alternative" character of the underground press is expressed by the type of news it printed and the nature of its interpretation. The issues that were the focus of attention in the underground media were subject to change, but while they attracted attention, they constituted the "causes" on which the media based their reason for being. Opposition to the Vietnam War had been one of the movement's principal causes, although the underground media originated in the enigmatic free-speech movement that flared briefly on the West Coast at UCLA in the early 1960s. On the East Coast, disarmament served as the focus of SDS (Students for a Democratic Society) in its early days. Both of these groups emerged suddenly, just before the height of American involvement in Vietnam, and later dissolved into the amorphous, all-encompassing "movement." With the Vietnam War over, with abortion sanctioned by the Supreme Court, and with military conscription at an end, there was no future for the "movement" and its media. These were their major causes. Being anti-establishment ceased and these youth *became* the establishment.

The underground media were a phenomenon of some importance and warrant closer scrutiny, particularly when considering such issues as media influence and media control.

Those underground media with the largest circulation were the ones with the greatest preoccupation with sex. For this reason, the *Village Voice* (120,000), *Los Angeles Free Press* (95,000), *Berkeley Barb* (85,000), and *East Village Other* (65,000) carried extensive classified ads devoted to sexual matters. The big underground papers on the West Coast had a greater preoccupation with sexual deviation than those in other parts of the country.

The underground newspapers with a substantially smaller circulation, such as the *D.C. Gazette* (5,000), *Quick-Silver Times*
(20,000), *Harry* (12,000), and *Off Our Backs* (5,000), carried very
few, if any, sex ads.

There was also a "class" distinction among some of the
underground newspapers. The *Berkeley Barb* (today defunct) was
essentially an underground tabloid. In one edition, eight of its
20 pages were devoted to sex ads. The balance of the paper
consisted of sex-related articles and very brief pieces on standard
underground themes. Its nearby competitor, the *Los Angeles
Free Press*, on the other hand, conveyed the tone of underground
"establishment." Its format was more conventional and its
articles were longer, better written, and covered a wider range
of subjects than did those of the *Barb*. A similar relationship
was evident among the big underground newspapers on the East
Coast, where the *Village Voice* was, and still is, underground
establishment, catering to the liberal intellectuals. The now-
defunct *East Village Other* played the role of the tabloid, catering
to underground anti-intellectuals.

The Underground News Collectives

The high degree of uniformity amid the diversity that typified
the underground press was attributable to the presence of
underground news services. There were four major coordinating
services—Liberation News Service (LNS), Underground Press
Syndicate (UPS), Cooperative High School Independent Press
Service (CHIPS), and College Press Service (CPS)—that acted
as an interchange among the hundreds of underground media.
They also provided original material much of which found its way
into the otherwise independent local underground outlets.

The Underground Press Syndicate and the Liberation News
Service were the major news services of the general underground
press. CHIPS and CPS performed the same function for the
underground high school and college presses, respectively. Both

in their tone and in their objectives, LNS and UPS differed markedly.

LNS operated out of a large basement with an offset printing press located one block from the Columbia University campus in New York City. It obtained its principal financial backing from donations. A major donor was the Joint Council of Churches. A "collective" of eight white young men and women ran the service. Three coordinating editors, appointed from the collective every two weeks on a rotating basis, managed the writing and selection of articles for biweekly, ten-page packets sent to a mailing list that, it is claimed, numbered 600 subscribers, including most of the underground newspapers. The biweekly packets that LNS distributed lacked the vitriolic tone, adolescent vocabulary, and four-letter words that typified the underground media it serviced. The articles were generally well written, reproduced by photo offset from typed manuscript and printed on large 11-by-16-inch sheets.

The thrust of the material was political, the focus on anti-war issues, racial and economic injustices, and feminist themes. If at all possible, the injustices were linked in one way or another to U.S. policies, domestic or foreign. The members of the collective who were interviewed by the author viewed the United States as the "enemy of the world" and expressed strong sympathy for the socialist and communist systems. They were radicals rather than revolutionaries, since they looked to education and evolution as the means of achieving the universal collectivization that they admired.

The bias of this news service (and of the underground press in general) was apparent from what it chose *not* to report. The LNS ignored the Russian repression of Soviet intellectuals and the considerable *underground* literature there. The service did not carry a single article on the Soviet show trials of Jews, their cultural repression by Soviet authorities, or the protests in the United States and Russia regarding Soviet treatment of Jews.

In domestic matters, problems of welfare did not attract the attention of LNS (or the underground in general), nor did the problems of the sociology of poverty or the education of the poor. The LNS packets and the underground media focused in general on identifying and reporting discontent, rather than its solution.

UPS was the other major news service serving the general underground media. It provided a free biweekly packet to 200 underground newspapers. It was operated by three women, 22 to 25 years old, one of whom was a college graduate. As at LNS, all were white. UPS operated from a loft in the Union Square section of Manhattan. The UPS editors were devoted principally to the cause of feminism. Indeed, they saw this issue as taking precedence over all others. In political matters they favored collectivism. However, unlike LNS's affection for socialism, UPS representatives favored no government at all. Their millennium was anarchy.

In style and content, UPS differed markedly from LNS. UPS employed the vitriol and four-letter words that typified their subscribers' writing styles. Their articles were brief, nasty, and generally lacking in substance.

The UPS loft served as a residence for its editors, who, like the LNS group, drew small sums for their own support. UPS obtained its principal financial backing from the Bell & Howell Corporation. This was facilitated through an arrangement whereby UPS collected copies of all underground newspapers for microfilming by Bell & Howell, which then sold the microfilm to libraries and split the fees 50–50 with UPS.

UPS, which claimed a combined *readership* (as distinct from circulation) of 6 million, also operated the Free Ranger Advertising Coop, which served as an advertising representative for over 100 underground newspapers. UPS claimed to have obtained over $200,000 in national ad revenues for the underground media in the 1968–71 period. This was in addition to the ad revenues obtained by underground newspapers locally.

How to Start a High School Underground

In a booklet by the above title, Cooperative High School Independent Press Service (CHIPS) introduced the high school reader to the spirit of the "movement":

> Some [students] are dropping out of school, others are burning down their schools and many are starting underground papers. While all three of these things are quite commendable, this booklet is only about the last one—starting an independent paper at a public high school.

After a competent description of methods to be used in staffing and printing the paper, the booklet advocated distribution of the underground newspaper on the school's grounds rather than in the school's general area. This is designed as the staff's first confrontation with authority and a step in its radicalization.

> The [school] administration knows that if the paper is underground, they have absolutely no control over it, and that scares them. So they set up little "conditions" for approval, hoping to at least be able to exercise some control over it. Of course you will have to consider local circumstances. In general I would suggest that you tell the school board to take their compromise and shove it up their ass. You shouldn't have to compromise your rights.

As its principal service, this high school press syndicate distributed a biweekly packet consisting of 16 pages of mimeographed news and commentary, for which their 60 subscribing publications paid $4 a year.

The following are titles of some of the news articles contained in a packet. The articles were intended for reproduction by subscribing high school newspapers:

> Bugs Pop Up Everywhere
> Army Files on High School Students Uncovered
> Principal Rips Off Angela
> Teachers Suspended for "Disorderly Conduct"

Mayday: A Brief Listing of Events
Students Force Resignation of Principal
Sex Discrimination Opposed in Little League
Principal Attacked for Racial Work
Teacher Dismissed as Being Witch
Principal Fined for Hair Expulsion
Files Reveal Wide Range of Groups Being Spied On

One CHIPS news packet carried an article that began: "The Student Information Center is in the process of putting together a pamphlet on birth control and abortion for *high school aged women.* . . ." In another article in the same issue, an upstate New York youngster solicited for "ideas on underground activities," in which he included an example: "Wanted: different methods of destruction against society if retaliation is needed, such as starting thousands of fires during the dry season in wooded sections."

The coordinating group at the next level of education was *College Press Service*. It had an audience consisting of about 300 college newspapers, most of which were not part of the underground establishment but were papers supported by college funds. In addition, about 20 conventional undergrounds subscribed to this service. The CPS editorial staff consisted of four persons in a Washington, D.C., office and a few correspondents located in different cities and campuses. Three correspondents were reported to be resident abroad, one each in Paris, Saigon, and Beirut.

CPS performed the same basic exchange and editorial functions for the college media as CHIPS did for the high school media. CPS, however, distributed its eight-page packets twice a week and charged, but didn't always collect, between $50 and $450 a year for the service. Its materials were printed on its own offset equipment. In spirit and tone the CPS material was more restrained and thoughtful than its high school counterpart. Its articles generally were lengthy discussions of significant issues.

Included in one packet was a long exposé on classified research at UCLA, written by an associate professor of philosophy there. CPS also informed its subscribing newspapers how to charge someone else's telephone when making long-distance calls, and provided feminist attacks on the male sexual ego.

The Cost of Entering the Underground

The underground media taught an important lesson about freedom of entry into the field of mass communications. A newspaper of relatively modest circulation (say, less than 100,000) could be published at very nominal cost. This was made possible by the photo-offset process, which involved the "photographing" of typed pages, pictures, and sketches. The newspaper could be prepared for the printer simply by pasting typed text and photographs on an ordinary sheet of paper. The cost of a photo-offset newspaper averaged approximately $1 per page for every 250 copies. Thus, a run of 10,000 copies of an eight-page edition would cost less than $350, plus a nominal charge for machine-folding of the newspaper. Color printing added to the cost.

This investment could generate a gross revenue of $1,000 to $2,500 for newspapers selling at 10 to 25 cents a copy. This income was generally split with the vendor. Advertising by local boutiques, record companies, movie theaters, water bed salesmen, and bookstores brought in additional revenue.

Since the staff, consisting of a handful of students or recent graduates, generally worked without pay or for pocket money, labor was also a modest expense. However, there was almost always a deficit, since not all copies were sold and there were overhead expenses such as rent, heat, electricity, telephone, postage, and supplies. Nevertheless, the underground press showed that the economic requirements for publishing a newspaper need not be a matter of real concern for those intent on communicating their point of view.

With a relatively modest investment totaling about $2,000, it was possible to purchase equipment such as an IBM electric typewriter with a number of interchangeable typefaces, a headline machine to produce large, bold type, and art equipment—all of which, together with the photo-offset process, could render a professional-looking product. Today the task is even simpler, as computers produce the entire product, including headlines.

Some of the underground newspapers were distributed free of charge (as are many establishment weeklies). They relied on advertising or local donations. Similarly, some of the smaller underground newspapers did not charge for classified ads. The inability of most of the papers to guarantee a minimum circulation or even to be certain of a regular publication schedule precluded them from attracting national or regional advertising revenue on a major scale. In several instances in which these requirements were met, the underground paper became a successful economic operation.

Of the 79 newspapers subscribing to the Underground Press Syndicate in 1968 (increased to 130 in 1971), 28 percent reported that they were profitable. The other 72 percent were breaking even or losing money. The aforementioned Glessing study reported that the *Berkeley Barb*, owned by Max Scherr, had a profit of $265,000 in 1969. A large part of this profit, however, was due to a salary scale in which staffers received $1.65 per hour and the editors received "nominal weekly wages." When the fact that the owner was earning $5,000 a week became known, most of the staff resigned. That this degree of exploitation of "turned-on" youth was possible must say something about their credulity.

Testing the Establishment

By pressing up against the bounds of convention, the underground media and youth culture subjected the First Amendment to considerable pressure. Whereas the government had the power to censor only in the field of broadcasting, the pressure of the counterculture on convention succeeded in weakening the government's will to protect the freedom of the press. The *Los Angeles Free Press*, which had an audited circulation of 95,000—one of the largest weeklies in the nation—was indicted after it published the names of state undercover narcotics agents in California. The list, including home addresses and telephone numbers, appeared under the headline "There Should Be No Secret Police." The names of the undercover agents had been obtained from a former mail clerk in the state attorney general's office. Drugs were one of the counterculture's "causes," a factor that was to raise havoc in the ensuing decades.

Publication of the roster was not in itself illegal. But, after a long deliberation, the jury convicted the newspaper for being a "fence" under the stolen goods statute. The editors could have received a sentence of up to 19 years in prison. The State Supreme Court reversed the lower court's decision on the grounds that the editors did not know that the information was stolen.

The implications of the lower court's decision for the establishment press were far-reaching, and received the immediate attention of a three-column analysis in the *Wall Street Journal*.[3] Said the article: "If this decision is not overturned by a higher court it will force the establishment press to limit its sources of information, censor itself and be more hesitant in exposing government malfeasance."

Just a year earlier, another court, faced with precisely the same type of situation, drew a different conclusion. Senator Thomas Dodd lost a similar case involving columnist Drew Pearson, who published documents stolen from the senator's files. In the *Free Press* case, however, the defendant was not a powerful member of the establishment, but a medium continually at odds with the authorities.

The Drug Lyric Affair

The underground media involved broadcasting as well as newspapers. Here, too, the basic freedoms were tested.

As was its custom every Wednesday, the seven members of the Federal Communications Commission met in its private chambers on February 24, 1971, to deliberate on matters brought before it by the FCC staff. Several months earlier, the Department of the Army had made a presentation to the commission regarding its concern over the broadcasting of songs that tended to glorify the use of drugs. The commission now voted—five in favor, one opposed, and one abstaining—to release a public notice that

> relates to a subject of current and pressing concern: the use of language [lyrics] tending to promote or glorify the use of illegal drugs. . . . The licensees [of broadcasting stations] must make the judgment and cannot properly follow a policy of playing without someone in a responsible position knowing the content of the lyrics. . . . Such a pattern of operation . . . *raises serious questions as to whether continued operation of the station is in the public interest.* In short, we expect broadcast licensees to ascertain, before broadcast, the lyrics or words of recorded musical or spoken selections played on their stations.[4]

The implications of this public notice were profound: first for its origin, a presentation made by the U.S. Army;[5] second, for its threat to revoke a broadcast license when the commission's (or the military's) judgment on broadcast content was not adhered to; and third, for its revelation of how uninformed the government was regarding the scope and development of the underground.

This challenge made strange bedfellows. Almost immediately, a number of major broadcast groups—including RKO General, a subsidiary of General Tire that was a major defense contractor, and Pacifica Foundation, a radical noncommercial broadcast group—filed a joint appeal with the FCC for reconsideration of this policy. As a result, the FCC tempered its public notices to suggest that it was merely highlighting an already inherent part of licensee obligation. But the public notice was not withdrawn, and the government's position that it could exercise its authority over program content was advanced another step.

In the one dissenting opinion, Commissioner Nicholas Johnson noted that "drug abuse *is* a serious problem [but] not merely among the young," The commissioner's dissent called attention to songs that glorified the use of alcohol, and pointed out that there were more alcoholics in one city, San Francisco, than there were narcotics addicts in the entire nation.

Commissioner Johnson concluded that the other commissioners were really joining in an attempt to repress the youth culture. He saw this as a "thinly veiled political move." To illustrate his point, Johnson revealed that many of the song lyrics singled out as objectionable by the Army were not related to drugs but rather to social commentary, such as:

> *Itemize the things you covet*
> *As you squander through your life.*
> *Bigger cars, bigger houses,*
> *Term insurance for your wife.*

Investigating College Radio

Three weeks after issuing the order regarding drug lyrics, the FCC launched a comprehensive investigation of college radio stations.

Of the more than 2,300 institutions of higher education in the United States, nearly half have their own radio stations. These stations include high-powered facilities that broadcast to the local community, low-powered stations (10 watts or less) whose signals are confined to the local campus, and a strange breed called the "carrier current" facility. The first two types operate under noncommercial licenses regulated by the FCC. As licensees, they are subject to the FCC's rules. But the third type of facility, the unlicensed carrier current service, has not been significantly controlled by the commission.

Approximately 450 colleges and universities operate *unlicensed* radio facilities in the carrier current radio service. The radio signals used in this service are conducted along the electric power distribution wires into and among buildings on the campus. The radio signals "leak" from the wires and can be picked up by regular radio receivers located in close proximity, without the need to be attached to the distribution system. Another unique feature of this type of college radio service is that it may carry advertising; the other categories, as already noted, operate under noncommercial licenses.

Ostensibly in response to several inquiries from carrier current college stations for permission to extend their coverage beyond the campus, the FCC, on April 4, 1971, issued a questionnaire to all college radio stations operating in the carrier current service. The questions included a request for information regarding news and editorial policy, financing, and distribution of revenues.

Again, the dissenter was Commissioner Nicholas Johnson. Among his reasons were: the nearly complete absence of complaints regarding campus radio stations; the fact that the questionnaires were not restricted to stations that were requesting permission to go off campus but were sent to all carrier current college stations; and the fact that there was evidence of political intent in the investigation. In circulating the original materials on this subject among the commissioners, members of the FCC staff had added an appendix containing articles from *Newsweek* (May 18, 1970) and *Parade* (May 31, 1970) that warned of the political content of college media broadcasts. The commissioners were again stampeded by the Pentagon—an interaction potentially as dangerous to establishment media as it was to underground media.

The commissioners supporting the inquiry joined in a rather ingenuous statement that began: "Campus radio [should] grow and add diversity to our method and content of information. [We] hope college students could appreciate our awareness of their growing importance."

The absence of deliberative judgment in these matters is apparent from the fact that the FCC did not have to launch a federal investigation to obtain the information it desired. The Corporation for Public Broadcasting (CPB) had released a comprehensive study of this subject just 18 months earlier.

The CPB survey found that most college radio stations obtain the bulk of their financing from student activity funds. The average budget ranges between $16,000 a year for carrier current stations to $47,000 for the high-powered noncommercial college stations. Only the carrier current services had advertising income. The average station earned about $5,300 a year from these advertisements. To aid them in obtaining commercial revenue, the carrier current stations were serviced by a number of national sales representatives, such as the National Student Marketing Corporation, Campus Media, Inc., and Rock Media, Inc.

The CPB study also reported that college radio stations were an important training ground for the broadcasting industry. It was found, for example, that the college stations lost most of their staff members in their junior and senior years to local commercial broadcasting stations. A tabulation based on a sub-sample of 63 of the responding colleges showed that, as a group, about 900 of their graduates enter the broadcasting profession each year.

Absorption

The underground media had not only provided a means of expression for radical and disenchanted youth, they had evolved into the experimental proving ground for the next generation of journalists, editors, and publishers.

Even before these young people had taken their place in the establishment, their techniques and their views had begun to appear in the establishment media. Many of the major media, broadcasting as well as print, subscribed to the underground news services; and some establishment journalists contributed articles to the underground press, generally under assumed names.

The adult community, meanwhile, accepted the youth culture's clothing and hair styles, vocabulary, and artistic and musical tastes. In addition, a significant number of planks from the underground's social and political platforms gained wide support, some finding expression in state and federal legislation. These include public policy in ecology and food safety, discontinuation of the military draft, reduction in the minimum voting age, and disengagement from the Vietnam War.

Most of these issues, though championed by the "movement," did not originate with it. Rachel Carson's 1962 book *Silent Spring* (Houghton Mifflin), conservation groups, outspoken staff members of the Federal Food and Drug Administration, and network television provided the major impetus in making the public aware of the problems surrounding the quality of our environment and purity of our food and water. Similarly, major advances in civil rights were achieved in the first half of the 1960s before the youth rebellion began. Nor can Kate Millett, Germaine Greer, or their sisters in the feminist movement be described as members of the youth culture. The anti-war movement in its early stages, the use of drugs by white middle-class youth, experiments in communal living, and unstructured school programs were the principal planks in the underground platform that were more distinctly their own.

It was the toleration and partial acceptance by the adult community of many of the "movement's" views that constituted the principal external threat to the future of the underground media, and to the youth culture. The ability to shock has been reduced with time and exposure. And as the views, lifestyle, appearance, and values young people advocated gained acceptance, their uniqueness and eccentricity were eroded. Evidence of the demise of the "movement" was the return of college youth to beer and old-fashioned antics.

By incorporating eccentricity into the system, the establishment renders the eccentric predictable and, therefore, acceptable. Kate Millett, Abbie Hoffman, and Allen Ginsberg became part of the entertainment world. Their image in the public mind was that of actors playing roles. Eventually, their identity as professional eccentrics replaced their ideas. As a sign of the times, Ginsberg eventually shaved off his beard and cut his hair. He did this just as sideburns and long hair made their appearance among the "hard hats" and in the halls of Congress.

It is also interesting to observe that the counterculture itself was not monolithic. The different groups constituting the "movement" advocated objectives that were often at cross-purposes. Thus, black women wanted to have the experience of staying at home and being supported by their husbands, while white wives strove for the reverse. Homosexuals demanded the right to be married and to be drafted into the military service, while young straights rejected both institutions. The anti-war groups stressed the sanctity of life, while the same white middle-class suburbanites and their radicalized youngsters advocated free and uncontrolled abortion. In the final analysis, freedom of the press survived the counterculture.

9 The Entertaining Medium

The Task Facing Management

The programming demands placed on television are probably beyond its capacity to meet. TV is expected to be all things to all men. It serves as a supplement and sometimes even a substitute for movies, newspapers, novels, magazines, the theater, the town meeting, and the local school system. Moreover, it has to appeal to all levels of sophistication and taste. Its stories are expected to have the mass appeal of the old dime novel and the sophisticated plotting of *The Spy Who Came In from the Cold*. Its talk shows must possess the fascination of the old gossip columns and at the same time have the redeeming value of group therapy. The children's programs must replace an older generation's "Perils of Pauline" while coming to the rescue of the local school system. Its news coverage is expected to combine the comprehensiveness of the *New York Times* with the intimacy of a small-town weekly. This is no mean feat. Indeed, it is virtually impossible.

Today's radio broadcasters have managed to get around similar demands in part by limiting themselves to a specific format such as soul music, or classical music, or simply news and weather. But they have mainly passed the buck to television.

Television programs, however, are costly—too costly to be effectively produced even by a group owner. Only by showing programs to the combined audiences of a hundred or more television stations, as the networks do through their affiliates, can the cost of expensive talent, staging, taping, and selling to advertisers be made into a profitable business. The *size* of the audience is what counts, and here lies the root of nearly all criticism of television programming.

Television's critics argue that one need not sacrifice quality for popularity. And of course, it is true that some children's programs that edify also manage to keep the child's attention. *Sesame Street* has proven that. For the most part, however, audience surveys show that, even among adults, good solid drama, in-depth news programs, and sophisticated entertainment do not attract the largest audiences.

As an example, a half-hour program entitled *Escalation in Vietnam*, broadcast over the CBS Network attracted only 25 percent of the viewing audience, while a rerun of *Marcus Welby, M.D.*, broadcast by the ABC Network at the same time captured 41 percent of the viewing audience. Even the evening news broadcasts of all three networks combined attract, on the average, only one out of three households. Indeed, as a group, "informative" programs such as news, documentaries, discussions, and interviews *at best* attract half as many viewers as a mystery, Western, comedy, or variety show.[1]

This reality has created a growing and potentially dangerous tension between educated viewers and those who operate the television communications system. The educated, who are articulate and influential, are pressing for some restraint on the profit motive so that the medium will serve their tastes as well as those of the "mass man."

As a compromise, Congress created the Corporation for Public Broadcasting in 1967 and funds it annually. For their part, the commercial broadcasters are only too happy to have the intellectual market spun off, so to speak, if that means that there will be less objection to their own program fare. The high purchasing power of the educated has no special appeal for television advertisers. The sales appeal of soaps, beer, gasoline, deodorants, razor blades, dog food, and breakfast foods depends not so much on income as on age and sex.

Critics at Large

The attacks on network programming that hurt TV most come from 18- to 49-year-old women, the housewives and homemakers. They are the very core of the mass audience. They are the buyers of the products advertised on television. Their objection, however, is not to adult program fare but to what is and what is not being broadcast for their children.

An international survey of television programming shows that the United States is the only major country whose networks carry no weekday afternoon programs for children. At best, some local television stations run absurd and violent cartoons for the juvenile market.

Only the United States and Finland, according to another study undertaken by the National Citizens' Committee for Broadcasting, confine children's shows principally to Saturday mornings. Also, children's shows carry 16 minutes of commercials per hour, twice the number carried on adult programs.

The advertisers that would be most affected by a ban on children's commercials at the network level include: Kellogg, Mattel Toys, and General Mills. Together, these three corporations account for 25 percent of all children's advertising. Five other corporations—General Foods, Deluxe Topper, Quaker Oats, Miles Laboratories, and Mars, Inc.—account for an additional 25 percent. These eight corporations account for over half of the three networks' total revenue received for children's programs. In all, about 80 companies advertise on children's network programs.[2]

Who are the advocates for limiting free use of television? Surprisingly, it was the Westinghouse Corporation that first suggested limiting the networks' use of prime time. The attack on cigarette commercials was initiated by John Banzhof, a New York attorney. A group of Boston housewives calling itself Action for Children's Television (ACT) advanced a proposal for limiting advertising on children's programming, and the United Church of Christ successfully reversed an FCC decision to renew the license of station WLBT-TV on the precedent-setting grounds that the station ignored the local black population.

As we see, the principal advocates of greater government involvement in mass communications have been public interest groups, and in one instance a major corporation. These are all members of the establishment, not members of a radical counterculture. The objectives of these and other public interest groups are well intended and, for the most part, unselfish. It is for these reasons that they are successful.

But the profits earned in mass communication are the results of the media's ability to satisfy the demands of the majority. Public interest groups rarely represent the majority view in communications matters. Their goals must therefore be imposed by the government, with all that this means for the freedom of the press—a concern that exceeds in importance all the altruistic goals of public interest groups.

One of the central complaints underlying the protests of many public interest groups is the alleged unchanging character of television programming. It is their belief that government intervention is necessary to foster change. However, television programming has changed radically over the years. The problem is these changes have not been in the direction they would have wished. The changes that have taken place were the result of technological developments and the accompanying expansion of the audience. In effect, television in America had metamorphosed into the nation's principal mass medium.

Evolution of Television Programming

In its early days television was a local medium. The American Telephone and Telegraph Company, which provided the facilities that tied together hundreds of affiliated broadcasting stations into networks, did not complete construction of even the basic relay or "backbone" system until 1953. During this early period, most television programs were locally produced and live, or they consisted of old movies.

While AT&T's transcontinental video relay system was being expanded, network programs were transmitted live from studios in New York City. During this period the gross revenue of the networks increased from only $55 million in 1950, before transcontinental interconnection, to $233 million in 1953 after the first trunk line was completed. Twenty years later, with a fully developed network system, the gross revenue (before commissions) of the three networks exceeded $1.7 billion.[3] By 1988, it had reached $7.6 billion.[4]

The creation of a nationwide network of affiliated stations attracted national advertisers and provided the means of spreading the cost of programs among a large number of stations. The use of filmed and taped programs permitted the director greater flexibility in the use of both indoor and outdoor settings. In economic terms it provided the producer with the potential of future resale, generally referred to in the trade as "syndication." At that time there was a large market for reruns of the evening shows in the daytime hours, since in these early days the networks provided little daytime programming. Nascent foreign television services also came to rely on the American networks for low-priced syndicated programs. Table 10 lists the highest rated—i.e., the most popular syndicated programs—in 1987.

Table 10   Highest-Rated Syndicated TV Programs, 1987

	PERCENTAGE OF HOUSEHOLDS
Wheel of Fortune	19.0
PM Magazine	12.3
Jeopardy	12.1
Oprah Winfrey	10.5
Big Spin	9.9
Family Ties	8.0
People's Court	7.9
M.A.S.H.	7.5
Donahue	7.4
Win, Lose or Draw	7.0

Source: *World Almanac 1989*, Scripps Howard, New York, p. 357.

When the telephone company finally completed its nationwide video transmission system, north and south as well as east and west, it consisted of 96,000 channel miles of intercity relays connecting 400 commercial television stations in 217 cities. During the final phases of its construction, between 1953 and 1959, the number of television receivers in the United States doubled from 27 million to 55 million. This brought television into nearly 85 percent of the homes in the nation and supported a greatly expanded network schedule.

The character of the programming changed to meet the tastes of this mass audience. The wealthy and the educated were among the first to possess television. But as the price of television sets declined, the audience grew and its average level of education and wealth declined. The result was predictable: a gradual phasing out of the Sunday-afternoon cultural schedule and the discontinuance of such programs as *See It Now*, *The Voice of Firestone*, *Omnibus*, and a whole genre of program known as the television play, which for a number of years had been the dominant form of television entertainment. The talents who once wrote television plays—Reginald Rose, Rod Serling, Paddy Chayefsky, and others—left the medium to become prominent contributors to the stage and screen.

The directors of television plays were also newcomers, who have since left television and made their mark in another medium. John Frankenheimer directed the original television play "The Days of Wine and Roses" for *Playhouse 90* on October 2, 1958, at the age of 28. Since he has left television, he has directed such films as *The Manchurian Candidate, Grand Prix*, and *The Fixer*. Others of this caliber who worked in television in its early days and who have left the medium include Arthur Penn (*The Miracle Worker* and *Bonnie and Clyde*,) Norman Jewison (*In the Heat of the Night, The Russians Are Coming, Fiddler on the Roof*), Franklin Schaffner (*Planet of the Apes*), Sidney Lumet (*The Pawnbroker*), and others.

These talented artists complained that television had gradually evolved from the experimental medium it was in the 1950s into a tightly run commercial operation that was merely an extension of advertising. They also criticized the committee system, in which creative output was reviewed by business committees. This is the same criticism that used to be leveled at the movies when that medium was in the hands of the big studios. However, now that the movie industry is no longer a leading mass medium, *it* attracts the youthful experimenters and has become the status medium of the gifted.

Thus, the process of change has been present in television programming from the start, and without government prodding. The direction of this change has been away from the lofty, the enduring, and the profound as television has sought to bring pleasure to the mass audience. Public interest groups, almost by definition, are unsympathetic to mass tastes.

As technological changes converted television from an elite medium to a mass medium, its programming focused more and more on detective, espionage, adventure, and cowboy subjects as well as on situation-comedy series with canned laughter. Movies

made especially for television were introduced in the late 1960s.
They were often lengthy pilots that might or might not turn into
a series. But special television films have yet to approach the
quality of the early television plays. They more closely resemble
lengthy versions of the standard Western or detective series that
are now basic television fare. In effect, the old "dime novel"
is presented on TV, in a number of different formats. More
recently, television has drifted into what might be termed "social
worker" themes. These include such subjects as battered wives,
drug addiction, drunken driving, and the problems of working
mothers.

Program Turnover and Strategy

The sensitivity of television programming to popular tastes
is most apparent in the turnover of television programming.
Broadcasting magazine made a survey of the programs televised
during the 1971–72 season, the first under the FCC rule limiting
the networks to three of the four prime-time hours (7–11 P.M.).
As a result of this rule, the three networks provided 66 programs;
the survey found that 25 were *new*. As shown in Table 11, of the
41 "old" programs, only three survived from the 1950s. Twenty-
eight programs survived through the 1960s, but six of these were
movie programs. Thus, excluding the movies, only 22 of the 66
programs on the air in the fall of 1971 survived the 1960s. In
effect, over 40 percent of the programs on the air that season
were being shown for the first time. This rate of turnover is not
at all unusual for television.

   Now, the principal factor determining the survival of a network
show is the relative size of its audience. And for this information,
the advertisers and the networks rely on the audience measure-
ments of the A. C. Nielsen Company. Reliance on audience
ratings is analogous to maintaining a perpetual opinion poll regarding network programming and responding to the majority in
determining the network schedule.

Popularity with the audience and quality as defined by "experts" are often mutually exclusive. Therefore, a winner of the National Academy of Television Arts and Sciences award for the best comedy series, *My World and Welcome to It* (NBC), disappeared from the network schedule the following season. The determining factor in network decision was the program's relatively low audience rating (percentage of homes tuned in).

In more recent years, television audience research has involved, in addition to the rating, an increasing concern for the demographic characteristics of the viewing audience, specifically their age and sex. Does this portend a greater interest in sub-audiences? If programming for such sub-audiences should replace the present goal of programming for the majority, then

Table 11 Age of Network Television Shows on the Air in Prime Time, 1971–72 (three networks combined)

YEAR PROGRAM FIRST INTRODUCED	NUMBER OF PROGRAMS
New 1972	25
1971	3
1970	7
1969	9
1968	6
1967	3
1966	2
1965	3
1964	2
1963	0
1962	1
1961	1
1960	1
1950s	3
Total no. of programs	66

Source: *Broadcasting*.

women 18 to 49 years of age would probably become the main target of network programs, since they are the major spenders for those types of goods that lend themselves to nationwide advertising. A shift of this sort, however, could increase the number of persons unhappy with television programming because the tastes of subgroups differ sharply from the aggregate mass audience. A few years ago, for example, at least six (one-third) of the most popular programs for the entire audience failed to appear among the 18 most popular program listed for women 18 to 49 years of age. Among the shows that would have been axed, if the latter rating had been followed, would have been those that were most popular with the general public.

Of course, a failing program is not always dropped. Sometimes, if the program's poor performance is attributed to another network's exceptionally popular offering, it is shifted to another time slot. If, however, the competition's offerings are also relatively unpopular, the decision is usually made to drop the failing program entirely. Such decisions are made periodically throughout the season. New shows are generally waiting in the wings, should an existing show fail to attract an adequate audience.

These decisions are made on the basis of an overall game plan. Network programming resembles a game of chess in which "counter-programming" and "audience flow" constitute the major strategies. Counter-programming means placing shows that are totally different from competing network programs opposite one another. Audience flow strategy, on the other hand, capitalizes on the general reluctance of television viewers to change channels. It seeks to capture the audience early in the evening and then to provide them with a sequence of programs that will not lead them to shift to another channel. In practice, this has resulted in evenings of very similar types of programs. For example, one Monday-night schedule might consist of two comedies and end with an upbeat "Monday Night Movie." If you liked the comedy, you stayed with the network all evening. Using a counter-programming strategy, another network might offer a series of adventure/excitement programs that same night, and capture an audience that preferred that type of program.

Cost of Programs

The television networks spend more money to produce a single hour of entertainment than the average television station earns, after taxes, in an entire year. By 1988, it cost about $1.5 million to produce an hour of entertainment. Sports programs, such as NFL football, cost much more.

With the pressure to maintain the mass audience for nation-wide advertisers increasing, due to the competition from new technology, it was inevitable that by the 1980s the soap opera would come to prime time. For some people this was hitting the bottom of the cultural barrel. *Dallas* and *Dynasty* were the hits in this category, and they did deliver the mass audience.

However, riding on the coattails of this format were high-quality mini-series: stories with an end. (Though it often required several nights or weeks to reach the end.) The subject matter of a mini-series was also generally more substantive than the never-ending major series. The longest mini-series was a 29-hour-long epic, Herman Wouk's *War and Remembrance*. With it, the ABC network lost about $35 million on what will probably be a television classic. It had recreated, as part of its story line, every colossal event in World War Two.

This was a record loss by a network on an entertainment program up to that time. The all-time record was for a sports program. ABC lost $65 million on the 1988 Winter Olympics. So perhaps quality entertainment is not to be blamed. Indeed, the blame was placed on the length of the series.

In contrast, another mini-series, *The Lonesome Dove*, made a $15 million profit for CBS. It ran for only eight hours. ABC spent $110 million to produce *War and Remembrance*, compared to CBS's $16 million for *The Lonesome Dove*: $2 million an hour for the financial winner versus $3.7 million an hour for the loser. But the final report is not yet in. The network may still be able to recoup its investment through the syndication market and videocassette sales.

Overall, one can get a feel for the taste of the mass audience from the average ratings by type of program, as shown in Table 12. Sports clearly is king with an average rating of 30. Major football games have received ratings as high as 45. News is low on the scale of preference; it averages only 12 percent of the households in the U.S. Programs like *Dallas* and *Dynasty* have been up in there in the high 20s. But it takes a great deal of money to produce these popular programs.

By 1989, each of the three television networks was spending an average of about $35 million *a week* for programming. This cost keeps rising. Between 1960 and 1970, the cost of producing a one-hour network program had climbed by about 100 percent. The average cost of producing an entertainment feature increased from $114,000 for a one-hour episode in 1960 to $211,500 in 1970. And, as already noted, to $1.5 million in 1989.

The cost of entertainment in 1989 stood in sharp contrast to the "good old days," when four years of *Bonanza* cost NBC a total of $52 million. The network now has a backlog of 400 episodes

Table 12   Television Programs' Popularity by Type (average rating)

TYPE	PERCENT OF HOUSEHOLDS
Sports	30
Major series	29
Specials	22
Mini-series	16
News	12
Soap opera	7
Morning news	4

Source: A. C. Nielsen, *Report on Television* (1987).

that it will bc sclling and reselling in the syndication market—
this, after having already cleared its investment in its first run on
U.S. television. *Bonanza* has been seen abroad in 89 countries,
including most of Western Europe and the Middle East, and parts
of Africa, Latin America, and Asia.

Syndication

The cost of a television program is recouped by the producer
from two sources: its lease to a network or broadcasters (who
in turn derive income from the advertising that accompanies its
showing) and the resale of the program after its first run. The sale
of reruns is called "syndication." The producer of the program
has nothing to do with advertising, which we discuss in some
detail in the next chapter. The sale of a program's reruns—its
syndication—is where the program producer generally makes his
profit.

But some programs cannot be sold for reruns. This is so
not because there isn't a market for them, but because their
"residuals"—that is, the fee received by actors or participants
each time their program is shown—are too high. This fee has
no relation to the price charged for the program on its resale,
nor to the number of buyers, nor the success or failure of each
customer in obtaining advertising to accompany the program's
second showing. The residual is fixed obligation, part of an
original contract under which the talent was hired.

A single program of a variety series like the *Ed Sullivan
Show* has so many different performers that the residuals are
prohibitively high. This is why the immense backlog of decades
of "Ed Sullivan Shows" will probably never be rerun. A single
one-hour program that might have cost $155,000 for the original
showing could cost, on rerun, as much as $50,000 for residuals
alone. Programs, moreover, are not sold one at a time, but for a
season of several weeks. Thus a 13-week package in which each
hour had a residual of $50,000 involves a $650,000 commitment

on this one expense item alone. And these residuals will have to be paid for the *entire* package regardless of whether one or one hundred stations buy it, and the residuals are only part of the cost in marketing a rerun.

The high risk of syndication explains why some independent producers, when they signed a contract with a network for a new series, preferred to relinquish all rights to a show's future earnings in return for a guarantee covering production costs plus a percentage for profits. On the other hand, if an independent producer believed he had a show that would hold up for more than one season, it was worth his while to try to hold on to the rights, even if this meant losing money initially. Some production companies have been able to survive on the returns from reruns of shows like *Bewitched* and *Father Knows Best.* This type of show incurs much lower residuals than do the variety programs. A series with just one or two principals in the cast would incur residuals that are more manageable. Figures on the syndication industry are not prepared by a central source. They emerge from time to time from special presentations to the FCC.

All in all, about 80 percent of the networks' regularly scheduled prime-time programming is eventually available for syndication. However, as the networks expand their broadcast schedules, the television stations have fewer time slots in which to run syndicated programs. In recent years, network schedules have been expanded from seven to ten hours a day. True, the shrinking syndication market among affiliated stations is somewhat offset by the growing number of unaffiliated stations, currently numbering about 600. However, most of the unaffiliated stations lack the financial resources necessary for them to become a major market for syndicated programs. Before long, old programs may be less a sales problem than a storage problem.

Several rules-of-thumb apply to this field: It takes two to three years on the network for a show to pay for itself and to start clearing a profit for the producer. If a series doesn't hold up that long, syndication is its last chance to make money. If the show,

market and from local advertisers. At these levels there is not the slightest possibility of exerting pressure upon the medium to alter the content of the programs shown, since these are all taped or filmed by independent producers for nationwide distribution. It is not technically feasible for a local broadcaster to regularly insert or remove scenes or comments from programs that he leases for local showing, or in one that is coming through the interconnection facilities of the networks. What the local broadcaster can do is refuse to carry a network show or refuse to lease a program from the syndication market. But when this is done, it is to appease the tastes and biases of the local audience—with the encouragement of the government—and not in response to an advertiser's commercial or political interests.

Another myth is that television broadcasting, more than any other industry, can *afford* to be more public-spirited and that its use of the public airwaves places the industry in debt to the commonweal. However, a great many industries use publicly financed or publicly owned facilities. This is true of the trucking industry, which uses tax-supported highways; the airlines, which use publicly financed airports; the farming sector, which is heavily subsidized with public funds; and the petroleum industry, which enjoys special tax privileges.

The other notion, that television broadcasting is unusually profitable, is not supported by the evidence.

We can get a perspective of the profitability of the industry if we compare the profits of the three major television networks (ABC, CBS, NBC) with the earnings of individual industrial corporations. In 1988 there were 52 individual industrial companies that *each* earned more profits than the three networks combined.

All in all, as already noted elsewhere, while the television broadcasting industry can boast of a few examples of fantastic profits among its television broadcasting stations, the industry as a whole does not stand out as particularly profitable, certainly not enough to suggest that it is its duty—more than that of any other industry—to finance the so-called "public interest," which is in reality a euphemism for special programming for special interests.

There is another more important consideration. It is a mistake to look upon television and other mass media as simply another industry. Economic threats to the unhindered freedom of the mass media—implied in the demands for more public interest programming—could very easily redound to the public's greater loss, should they result in a mass communications industry beholden to the government for its economic well-being. At that point, an important part of the American political system, which depends upon continuous public scrutiny and surveillance of government, will have been rendered inoperable.

Deception Is Assumed

The third argument underlying hostility toward advertising is the feeling that it is all too frequently deceptive and misleading.

Among the classic deceptions disclosed by the media themselves was the Colgate-Palmolive commercial that purported to show sandpaper being shaved using its Rapid Shave Cream. In fact, the sand was mounted on plexiglass, since real sandpaper would have had to be soaked over an hour in the shaving cream in order to come clean. Then there was the case of Libby-Owens-Ford, which televised an open window to show the clarity of its glass. General Electric advertised its 10-inch color television set as "only half the price of many color sets"—its 10-inch set sold for $197. However, GE's 25-inch console sold for $499. "The latter," testified a straightfaced GE executive "is obviously more than twice as expensive."

Then there are the low-keyed deceptions consisting of such ambiguous slogans as: "99 and 44/100 percent pure." (Pure what?) "There's nothing like [product]." (It's that terrible?) "[Product] as only [company] makes it." (The others make a better product?)

Actually, the public is far less naive regarding advertising claims than the concern of consumer protection groups and government agencies would lead one to believe. The number of products and political candidates that have failed despite well-planned and well-financed campaigns is legion. In addition to a natural skepticism, the public is frequently entertained by public and private exposure of just such advertising deceptions. These exposes, as already noted, generally appear in the very media that benefit from advertising.

As a matter of fact, few of the slogans, product endorsements, and demonstrations are really intended to convince the consumer of a product's superiority. Rather they attempt to establish public familiarity with a new brand of a product that is usually bought casually, such as soap, cereal, or coffee. For well-established brands, the ads seek to associate them with an "image" or state of mind like wealth, status, virility, or good times. In this context, deceptiveness in advertising is relatively inconsequential, if not meaningless.

In most mass-marketed items it is easy to shift from one brand to another, for the products do not last long. Hence, even the most flagrant deceptions are not a serious social problem. On the other hand, items that are expensive and that last long are much more likely to be closely inspected by a prospective purchaser. Whatever glowing descriptions may be published in advertisements regarding houses, expensive clothing, automobiles, and the like, they are almost always tested by the purchaser's own observation and inspection.

The current feeling that advertising should be more truthful, if not actually informative, reflects a fundamental misunderstanding regarding its function. In part, this can be traced to the changing character of the advertising profession.

In the last three decades, advertising expenditures have increased enormously, rising fourfold. There has also been a parallel growth in the size of advertising agencies. Several have even gone public and are listed on the stock exchanges. The result is a widely held belief that advertising is an industry, indeed a growth industry. From this follows a fundamental misconception: that ads are products of this industry and that they, therefore, should be truthful in the same way that one would expect recently purchased food to be fresh or recently purchased appliances to be in good operating condition. Advertising, however, is not the product of a special industry, nor can advertising be an objective source of consumer information. It is merely old-fashioned salesmanship on a mass scale, and it is as much an integral part of the manufacturer's operations as is his shipping department. Its point of view, therefore, is *necessarily* biased.

No company can realistically be expected to spend large sums of money to criticize or be "objective" about its own product. By its very nature, advertising deals in half-truths. It proclaims the favorable aspects of the product and is silent about the less favorable. This is a common practice in many walks of life. It is done when applying for a job, when preparing for a date, and when campaigning for political office, as well as when selling goods and services.

Advertising *harmful* products is not the issue, for in such circumstances it is not the advertisement that should be discontinued but rather the production and distribution of the product. Harmfulness aside, it is naive to expect producers to bare their souls by confessing to a competitor's advantages or their own inadequacies when selling an otherwise useful product.

Creating Wants

Another common complaint against advertising is that it sometimes causes people to purchase products they do not really need. To the extent that this is true (and this is not as easy as assumed), it amounts to a very pleasant type of tax. These purchases ultimately support the mass media by encouraging advertising expenditures. The alternatives would be government support of the media, which would also be obtained through taxation—but of the unpleasant kind. More important—and an aspect of government support we must never forget—is that it inevitably entails a constraint on our freedom of expression and on the availability of information.

This "expansion of wants" has another side to it. Classical economics assumed that there was an automatic demand for the output of industry—that the problem was simply one of bringing price and quantity into equilibrium. But this has proven to be unrealistic. Because of the immense productive capacity of modern industry, the consumer has to be induced to desire the goods and services he can produce in his role as a worker. Otherwise they pile up on the shelves and unemployment ensues. Advertising has become a particularly important link between mass production and mass consumption.

The Advertiser in Search of an Audience: Media Analysis

The image of the advertiser as a mind bender, possessing awesome power over the behavior of his audience, is a myth founded on the public's unfamiliarity with the processes involved. In fact, advertising is a highly risky business. Millions are spent in a single advertising campaign without the slightest knowledge, until considerably later, as to how many people even saw the advertisement, much less whether it was successful in terms of the advertiser's sales volume. It is much like fishing. You can bait the hook with the best lure and use the finest equipment, but unless you have chosen the right spot and the right time there might not be any fish in the area. And fishermen know well that even then, "they may not be biting."

Advertising therefore involves a perpetual search for the most efficient method to reach just those persons who are prospective customers. There is an implicit acknowledgment that a customer can rarely be made out of whole cloth. The prospective buyer is understood to be in the market looking for the product, and the principal task of advertising is to induce that prospective buyer to purchase the brand being advertised.

In selecting media, the advertiser's objective is to reach the maximum number of the right people, with the right frequency, and in the right mood or atmosphere (movies aren't advertised on the obituary page), for the lowest cost per thousand prospects.

Most media attract fairly well defined audiences. Thus, the audience of a local newspaper or television station is defined by its geographical location. Magazines designed for men or women define their audience by sex. Even programs on radio and television are able to offer advertisers access to fairly well defined audiences. Sports events (males); soap operas (female homemakers); cartoons (children); and rock music (teenagers) are all programs directed at sub-audiences.

The advertiser also has to determine the probability that his advertisement will be seen. There are studies of "page traffic" in newspapers for example, which show that the front page is read by 99 percent of readers while the back pages reach only 25 percent or 30 percent. Yet this 25-percent readership can be more significant than the 99-percent, if the advertiser is selling to a specific audience. To reach men he will use the sports section, to reach women he will use the food or fashion section. An independent research study undertaken for 30 newspaper markets revealed that as many as 80 percent of the women who read newspapers read the food section regularly, not occasionally.

The Cost of Advertising

It generally comes as a surprise to those unfamiliar with the processes involved that the advertiser knows what he is spending, but not what it is costing. The reason is that he has a budget for advertising so that he knows his dollar expenditures, but not until long after the ad or commercial has been released is he aware of the size of the audience that saw or heard his message. Thus, he doesn't know whether he paid $5 or $10 to reach a thousand prospective customers.

If the public rejects the program carrying his commercial, the advertiser takes a loss in the form of wasted advertising expenditures. If the program catches on or retains an already established popularity, he has been successful. In either case there is no certainty, and the risks can be very high.

Because of the risks involved, there are few sponsor-owned programs on the air today. Instead, as noted earlier, the networks buy or produce the program and then sell participating ads to several advertisers. This permits the advertisers to spread their risk by buying time in a number of different programs. The cost of air time is only part of the price paid for advertising on television, though it is the greater part of the cost. The other cost component is the commercial itself.

Another significant myth concerning advertising and the mass media is the belief that large advertisers receive substantial discounts to the disadvantage of their smaller competitors. In the early days of television, the networks sold air time only to advertisers who themselves supplied the programs. Under this type of arrangement there were volume discounts. But the discounts were only for the purchase of air time, and the programs were purchased by the advertiser directly from the program's producer. This was a carry-over from radio-network days. These discounts posed some serious anti-trust problems and were the subject of more than one Supreme Court ruling.

However, this issue has ceased to be a matter of concern because of the rearrangement of business relationships. For many reasons, some already discussed—including the rising cost and increasing length of programs, which increased the risks involved—advertisers today no longer supply their own programs, but purchase time in programs supplied by the networks. Under this new arrangement, referred to as "participations," there are no volume discounts by any of the networks.

The price of "participations" is usually finely tuned to the estimated value of the size and type of audience generated by a given program. These prices change quite frequently in response to changes in production costs and the size of the audience.

Varying prices are quoted for "participation" in the same program, but these variations are for different seasons of the year, in accordance with the audience's viewing patterns. Price lists are made widely available to the trade and the same prices are offered to all advertisers, regardless of size. If these listed prices are not validated in the marketplace—if the audience isn't what was expected—bargaining ensues and new prices are established. At intervals, new lists are prepared, reflecting both general market conditions and changes in the market's evaluation of individual programs, based principally on audience surveys.

While television's advertising rates were skyrocketing, the cost of newspaper advertising increased only slightly. The reason for the relatively slow rise in the cost of newspaper advertising can be attributed to the relative stability in operating costs faced by newspapers, the presence of alternative modes of reaching local consumers, and the predictable nature of the local market.

It is interesting to note that in the newspaper field it is frequently the giant national companies that pay a premium for advertising rather than the relatively small local businesses. Those firms who use the newspaper medium infrequently are charged 60 percent over and above the price paid by local advertisers who contract for newspaper advertising by the year. For this reason national advertisers prefer to employ "co-op" advertising, by which they share the advertising costs of the local merchant, thereby benefiting from the deep discounts that the latter receives from the local press.

Another unique feature of newspaper advertising is the classified ad. Today nearly 30 percent of all newspaper advertising revenue (about $19 billion) comes from this source. And its importance is growing.

The Structure of Advertising

Today, advertising accounts for approximately 75 percent of the revenue received by newspaper; the rest of their revenue comes from the sale of the newspaper itself. In the case of commercial radio and television, advertising provides nearly 100 percent of the revenue received. In return, advertisers receive 60 percent of all newspaper space (up from 40 percent in 1940) and about 17 percent of prime-time television (7–11 P.M.). In non-prime-time the Broadcasters' Code allocates to advertisers up to 26 percent of television time. As for radio, the Broadcasters' Code recommends that advertising not exceed 18 minutes per hour or 30 percent of air time. However, less than half of the radio stations in the country have agreed to be bound by the provisions of this voluntary code.

Improvements in mass communication have vastly accelerated the growth of advertising. Back in 1935, when even radio was in its infancy and the nation suffered from economic depression, *total* advertising expenditures in the United States were only $1.7 billion. By 1951 this sum had quadrupled. By 1960, when television was reaching into nearly 90 percent of the nation's homes, all forms of advertising in the United States totaled $12 billion. A decade later it exceeded $25 billion, of which the mass media accounted for over half. By 1988, it totaled $118 billion.

Following World War II, all forms of mass media were put to use to sell the vastly expanded output of the nation's farms and factories. Thus, contrary to widespread predictions, the boom in television did not doom radio but paralleled a period of unprecedented growth in radio broadcasting. Radio's advertising revenue doubled in the decade 1959–69 and went on to increase fivefold, 1969–89. This same period also witnessed unprecedented growth of advertising in newspapers and magazines.

As shown in Table 13, newspaper revenues from advertising kept growing even though newspapers now competed with televi-

Table 13 Trend of Advertising Revenue (billions of dollars)

YEAR	TOTAL	NEWSPAPERS	TV	RADIO	MAGAZINES
1989	$74.3	$32.4	$26.9	$8.3	$6.7
1969	12.1	5.8	3.6	1.3	1.4
1959	6.5	3.5	1.5	.6	.9
1949	3.0	1.9	—	.6	.5
1939	1.2	.8	—	.2	.2

Source: *Advertising Age* (May 14, 1990). Prepared by McCann-Erickson, Inc.

sion. Available data show that between 1969 and 1989 newspaper revenues increased more than fivefold, this despite the explosive growth of television. And newspapers' advertising revenues continued to exceed those of television even in 1989.

Aggregate data do not explain significant differences in the economic function of the different types of mass media. There are two basic markets to which advertisers address themselves. There is the local market and there is the national market. Local advertisers include the department stores, chain stores, supermarkets, automobile dealers, and the classified columns. Local markets accounted for $44 billion in all forms of advertising in 1990. National advertising, principally by manufacturers themselves, totaled $55 billion that year. Included in these figures are more than the conventional mass media. These figures include billboards ($1 billion), computerized mailings ($21 billion), and the yellow pages ($8 billion), as well as promotions and merchandising.

Table 14 lists the ten companies with the largest advertising budgets, and provides a profile of where they spend this money. Sear's catalogues do not appear in this list—which explains where much of their billion-dollar budget is spent. Billboards, mailings, and promotions account for much of the unlisted expenditures in Table 14.

Table 14 Leading U.S. Advertisers, 1988 (millions of dollars)

	TOTAL*	MAGS.	DAILIES	TELEVISION NETWORKS	CABLE	RADIO NETWORKS
Procter & Gamble	$1,435	86	640	456	27	13
Philip Morris	1,364	230	17	324	22	7
Sears	1,003	43	3	128	2	47
RJR Nabisco	935	135	37	155	10	4
General Motors	839	129	8	233	7	22
Ford	648	125	3	188	4	14
Anheuser Busch	643	18	1	177	19	16
McDonald's	592	1	0	193	1	0
K Mart	590	20	1	26	1	6
Pepsi	581	1	0	115	5	1

*Total also includes spot television, outdoor billboards, and promotional advertising not shown separately.

Source: *World Almanac 1989*, Scripps Howard, New York, p. 358.

Local advertising is the mainstay of American newspapers (Table 15). They received 63 percent of all local advertising expenditures in the United States in 1989, and local advertising accounted for 88 percent of newspaper advertising revenues. Conversely, national or nationwide advertising is the mainstay of television. It received 30 percent of national advertising revenue that year, and national advertising accounted for 70 percent of television revenues. This separation of purposes—newspapers for local advertising and television for nationwide advertising—explains their ability to thrive together. In effect, they do not compete.

Magazines are the second-most-important vehicle for national advertising. They received 21 percent of all national advertising revenue in 1989. They also doubled this income through subscription revenues. Radio, on the other hand, is a local medium. In 1989, it accounted for 15 percent of all local

Table 15   Sources of Advertising Revenue, 1989 (millions of dollars)

MEDIUM	NATIONAL		LOCAL	
Newspapers	$3,720	12%	$28,648	67%
Television	19,279	62	7,612	18
Radio	1,547	5	6,776	15
Magazines	6,716	21	—	—
Total	$31,262	100%	$43,036	100%

Source: *Advertising Age* (May 14, 1990). Prepared by McCann-Erickson, Inc.

advertising, compared to television's 18 percent. Fully 82 percent of radio's revenues are from local advertising.

An interesting aside is the extensive use of coupons distributed by package-goods marketers through newspapers and magazines. In 1989, they distributed 263 billion coupons. These coupons, if cashed in or used, had a value of $115 billion. Redemptions, however, ran at a rate of about 4 percent; they thus had an actual value of $4.5 billion. This is nearly half the sum spent on radio advertising that year, and nearly two-thirds the advertising revenue received by magazines.[2]

On Socially Constructive Paths

Advertising, as we have seen, is a complex institution of considerably greater importance than is generally recognized. Yet, private groups and public agencies today advocate government rules that would limit and regulate its activities. They are particularly intent upon reducing the interdependence between advertising and mass communications. This may be motivated, in part, by a lack of knowledge regarding the delicate market mechanisms that permit advertising to serve as the economic base of mass media in the United States. Unfortunately, there is more to this problem.

Reformers today have managed to wrap themselves in a cloak of sanctity that a previous age had reserved for clerics and theologians. In the process, they have created an intellectual environment that has imposed a litany of unquestionable premises upon matters of social, political, and economic importance. Thus, the belief that if one's aims are unselfish they are necessarily desirable is all too frequently the basis of the most questionable schemes "in the public interest."

How can anyone argue in favor of a self-serving institution such as advertising? In today's intellectual climate it is not only unfashionable and in bad taste, it is considered antisocial. Yet the truth of the matter is that the results of the policies advocated by public interest groups and government agencies in the field of advertising and mass communications pose a very serious threat to our political freedom.

In advocating control over advertising one is saying, in effect, that the public must be protected from the purveyor of goods. Yet the Constitution protects the purveyor of ideas. It does this on the assumption that the public is able to judge for itself what is good and what is bad—or, more important, it assumes that no one else is better qualified to do so without causing greater harm in the process. It is a very small step, however, from the assumption that the public is *economically* naive to the assumption that it is *politically* naive.

An example of the extreme to which our confidence in the public's good sense has taken us in noncommercial matters can be seen in an FCC ruling that refused to censor a white racist, J. B. Stoner, whose 30-second "spot" announcements over television and radio stations in Tennessee and Georgia could accurately be depicted as a very serious threat to the safety of our citizens. Stoner's "announcement," which the FCC did not consider to be a public menace, is quoted here: "The main reason why niggers want integration is because niggers want our white women. I am for law and order with the knowledge that you can't have law and order and niggers too."

The complaint against this announcement was made by a broadcaster, who argued that by compelling him by law to carry such an announcement the FCC makes the public think that a broadcaster will publish anything for money.

The FCC required that he carry the announcement because "the public interest is best served by permitting the expression of any views that do not involve a clear and present danger or serious substantive evil that arises from public inconvenience, annoyance, or unrest."[3]

It is difficult to see how one agency of government (FCC) exhibits such supreme confidence in the public's ability to absorb such a raw insult calmly (which, with hindsight, it in fact did) and another agency of government (FTC) shows such lack of faith in the public's ability to ignore a questionable sales pitch for deodorants and shaving cream.

Some government agencies tend to overestimate their own wisdom and to underestimate the ability of individuals to discriminate among the many appeals made to them. What is needed today is a new sense of modesty about the abilities of government bureaucracies and an awareness of the destructive power they wield. The government, after all, can litigate endlessly. It matters little to the FTC that the final determination of a case may take one, two, three, or more years as it goes through the full trial-appellate process. Yet such an ordeal of litigation can literally ruin an average business.

Today it is fashionable in some quarters to disdain advertising, and indeed there is much in advertising that merits disdain. But to demand perfection as the price of survival is to make a demand that no one is even capable of defining. As the FTC itself noted in its decision in the Pfizer case (1971): "Unfairness is potentially a dynamic analytical tool capable of progressively evolving application which can keep pace with a rapidly changing economy. Thus as consumer products and marketing practices change in number, complexity, variety, and function, standards of fairness to the consumer also change."

Fairness aside, history has shown time and again that however *crooked* a businessman or group of businessmen may be, the danger they represent to the pubic's welfare is but a fraction of the threat posed by a government that seeks to keep its citizens "on a socially constructive path."

It should be remembered that advertising revenue provides the means by which mass communications in the United States has secured its independence of thought and action. That is what makes the current trend toward increased government interference in advertising so disturbing. For what is ultimately at stake here is not the survival of advertising. What is at stake is our society's historical right to information completely free of government interference.

It may sound odd to associate liberty with commercial advertising, but they are, in the final analysis, closely related.

▌▌ Mass Media in Mass Education

Relative Efficiency

The nation's public educational system serves 35 million students from the primary grades through high school. The cost of educating these students is estimated at about $137 billion a year, which comes to about $3,700 per pupil. By comparison the mass-communications industry spends about $70 billion annually. With this sum newspapers, radio, television, and magazines serve approximately 240 million Americans. This is an average of about $291 for each member of the "audience."[1]

A large part of the very significant difference between the per-pupil cost of formal education and the per-person cost of informing and entertaining the public is the result of differences in technology. Formal education is still largely a personal process. Each class of students carries the cost of at least one teacher with supporting staff, the cost of school supplies, and its share of the cost of the school building, overhead, and, in many cases, transportation. Keeping the public informed and entertained, on the other hand, is accomplished by means of sophisticated cost-reducing equipment, including space satellites, microwave, broadcasting stations, low-cost and long-lasting television receivers, transistorized radios, and high-speed computerized presses.

There is also a very substantial difference in "reach." The educational establishment employs more than 2 million teachers, plus additional supporting staff, in order to reach some 35 million students.[2] The mass-communications industry, on the other hand, is able to serve 240 million people while employing only 485,000 persons in all its occupations. Thus, the average "reach" per employee in mass communications is about 495 persons, as compared to 17 students per teacher. Mass communications therefore has a reach that is about 29 times greater than that of the educational system. This differential goes a long way toward explaining the difference in their cost per person—for education costs about 12 times more per person served than does mass communications. Clearly, technology spells the difference. Can or should the technology of mass communications be applied to mass education? The question goes to the heart of the American approach to education, for here too we face the question "who controls these media?"

The Principle of Diversity

Ethnic and cultural diversity has long been the distinguishing feature of American society. The desire to preserve this diversity and the fear of domination by any one group has historically prevented the centralization of mass education. Today's nomenclature refers to this approach as "pluralism."

The identifiable geographic location of many ethnic groups (Swedes in Minneapolis, Irish in Boston, Poles in Pittsburgh, Italians in Providence) has helped mold the character of the American educational system, with its division into 15,700 relatively autonomous school districts nationwide.[3]

The size and number of these districts vary widely among the states. Hawaii, for example, has one school district while Texas and California each have over a thousand.

Efficiencies and cost economies of mass communications present a great temptation to educators—and taxpayers. There has, as a result, been a decided drift toward the use of the latest communications technology in American education. This raises some serious questions. Will the techniques of mass communications, when applied to mass education, change the basic diversity of our school system? If so, what are the long-range social and political implications? The answers to these questions are beyond the scope of this book. But an awareness of the forces that control the electronic instructional media is a necessary first step in evaluating their impact.

Public Television

Public television is aimed at an audience composed principally of people who wish to be informed as well as entertained. It is a medium that had its roots in "educational" television. More recently, it has been referred to as "public" or noncommercial television. The system receives its funds from federal grants, private donations, foundations, and recently has been permitted to broadcast advertising paid for by nonprofit organizations.

In 1967, Congress created the Corporation for Public Television (CPT) as the organization for channeling federal funds for the programming of ETV stations then being licensed by the Federal Communications Commission. For a number of years federal appropriations totaled $30 million, plus another $55 million to assist in the development of physical plant. Today the sum is about $185 million a year.

After years of fumbling and confusion, a sorting out has taken place, although the lines of responsibility and the path of funding are still confusing. Public broadcasting operations are today coordinated by the Public Broadcasting Service (PBS), which was established in 1969. It is best described as a communications cooperative, serving 338 member stations and an audience of about half of America's households.

PBS is owned and directed by its member stations, which themselves are accountable to their licensees. Public-owned stations have been licensed and are operated by community organizations (48 percent), universities (33 percent), and state or municipal authorities (19 percent).

The Corporation for Public Broadcasting, referred to earlier, receives federal funds and passes them on to the stations that support the acquisition services of PBS. In this way PBS—which is involved in coordinating the programming for nation-wide distribution—is supposed to be shielded from government intervention.

The public television system as a whole received from national, regional, and local sources in 1988 a total of about $1 billion. Table 16 provides a more detailed breakdown of its sources of revenue. About 45 percent of its financial support derives from personal and private business sources.

The Public Network

The PBS does not itself produce programs. It acquires them from the Station Program Cooperative, which is the framework through which public television stations cooperatively select and finance programs that will later be distributed by the PBS. The PBS also acquires programs from independent producers and from foreign sources, and makes them available through its satellite-interconnected system to its member stations. The cost of a program to any station is determined by the size of the station as well as the number of other stations making a commitment to purchase that program.

In 1989, PBS members were provided with nearly 1,600 hours of programming. About 50 percent of the programs distributed nationwide by the PBS were acquired from its member stations.

Table 16   Public Television Income, 1988

SOURCE	DOLLARS IN MILLIONS	PERCENTAGE OF TOTAL
Federal Government	$ 186	17%
Subscribers	242	22
States	210	19
Business	173	16
State Colleges	73	7
Foundations	43	4
Local Governments	39	4
Auctions	22	2
Private Colleges	16	2
Others	80	7
	$1,084	100%

Source: PBS Factsheet, 1990.

Another 30 percent were obtained from American independent producers and 12 percent from foreign producers. News coverage accounted for the balance. The character of public television programming outlined in Table 17 shows it to be quite different from commercial television.

The PBS has a staff of 310 located in Alexandria, Virginia, New York City, and Los Angeles. In addition to program acquisition and scheduling, the PBS provides audience research, and assists

Table 17   Character of Public Broadcast Programs

Public Affairs Science and Nature }	56%
Educational	22
Cultural	22
	100%

in revenue-producing activities for its members. Its own funding comes from member stations.

Public television became a nationwide network in 1978 when the PBS became the first television system to distribute its programs through satellite transmission. In 1984, the PBS purchased outright the four transponders it was using on Western Union's satellite. This provides the PBS with 178 down-links and 20 up-links.

Public television can, theoretically, be seen in 98 percent of the nation's homes. There are, however, several problems troubling the system. The first is the fact that most public broadcasting stations transmit on the UHF band, which provides poor reception. In many locations the cable system has saved the local station by carrying it into the area's homes, thereby improving its reception. However, if the cable doesn't carry the local public broadcasting station to the local subscribers, they cannot obtain it at all (their antenna has been removed).

Public Education

In addition to the standard program service provided by the PBS, about 250,000 students a year are enrolled in courses provided by its Adult Learning Service. This service, established in 1981, allows adults to take courses in the convenience of their homes. Videocassettes of 1,400 public television programs are also sold or rented to schools, libraries, and hospitals.

The PBS also provides instructional programs for use in elementary and secondary schools. About 80 percent of the public broadcasting stations provide educational programs for public schools. And nearly 30 million elementary- and secondary-school students attend schools served by public television stations. A special night service allows schools to record educational programs on their VCR for use at a time convenient to them.

The PBS's underutilized nationwide network and a growing crisis in American education may lead to a marriage of interests. The PBS is in search of revenue and the nation's school districts are in search of economy and efficiency. This can easily lead to a standardized, nationwide educational system based on public television. Indeed, the PBS is already actively involved in advocating the use of television technology in the classroom. In this lies a serious challenge to America's traditional aversion to standardization and nationwide centralization of significant social and economic institutions. It is an issue worthy of serious study, but it does not appear to have attracted much attention as yet.

From Field Publications come three widely distributed newspapers: *Weekly Reader, Read Magazine*, and *Current Events*; from Scholastic, Inc., come *Scholastic News, Junior Scholastic*, and *Scholastic Update*. And of course there are the school texts. It should be noted that printed matter presents less of a problem, however. It has generally been tailored to meet local needs. In addition, unlike educational television and educational radio, the printed media do not contribute to centralization of education, for they do not circumvent the classroom teacher. On the contrary, use of printed matter enhances the teacher's role, since he or she must be there to interpret its content. When using electronic media, however, the presence of a trained teacher is unnecessary; indeed, it would defeat the whole purpose of efficiency and cost saving offered by a "master" teacher located in a distant production center and able to serve a wider audience. Clearly, the outmoding of the classroom teacher poses a serious problem.

Yet the trend toward "electronic education" is getting little publicity. The proliferation of equipment and facilities has enabled state and federal authorities to program mass education of American students with little thought for the future of America's traditionally local approach to education.

Education Through Commercial Television

Two kinds of educational programs are shown on commercial television: (1) documentaries, which are often on prime time on commercial television and then loaned in film or tape for use by closed-circuit systems or by the PBS; and (2) experimental college-level instruction televised over commercial stations in the early-morning hours.

Loans of documentaries to educational facilities by commercial television have made a very small impact upon the educational market. The PBS reports that only 1.8 percent of their general programming and 0.3 percent of their ITV programming is obtained from commercial television.

As for instructional programming by commercial television, there have been only a limited number experiments with college-level instruction by commercial broadcast stations. In 1958, a nationally televised college-level physics course, *Continental Classroom*, went on the air, underwritten by foundation grants and carried by more than 150 NBC outlets at 6:30 in the morning. In subsequent seasons, courses in chemistry, math, and American government were also offered. Although more than 300 colleges cooperated in the program and viewing was said to be heavy, the program was dropped. The program *Sunrise Semester* was shown in several major metropolitan areas, but it remains an isolated experiment. Other than these examples, there has been no substantial attempt to televise instructional programs on commercial television.

Protests of numerous groups against the present style of children's programming on commercial television have focused attention on this segment of the program market. To date, however, the educational role of commercial programming can only be described as incidental.

Educational Radio

Although they are junior partners in the use of mass communications for education, educational or noncommercial (FM) radio stations are much more numerous than their television counterpart. The latest count (1989) puts their number at 1,370 or nearly four times that of public television stations. By comparison with the commercial radio stations in the United States, however, educational stations are the junior partner. In addition, many educational radio stations are, by and large, insignificant. One-third of them have an effective range of only two to five miles. Such short-range stations generally serve a college or university campus, which explains their ability to continue in operation despite their small audience (more often than not consisting of the school's dormitories).

Only one AM educational radio station is municipally owned (WNYC in New York City). The concept of community ownership simply does not exist in educational radio, as it does in educational television, where 25 percent of the ETV stations are community owned and 11 percent are owned by school districts.

Toward Consolidation

Contributing to the concern over future reliance on regional or national ITV for use in schools is the current trend toward administrative centralization of school districts across the United States, a trend that most educators agree will increase the overall efficiency of the system. If we go back to 1945, the trend appears particularly dramatic, the number of school districts having declined from 101,400 to the present 15,700 in less than 50 years.

Administrative centralization, however, should not be equated with standardization of curriculum. Indeed, teachers, traditionally a key influence on children, have increased in number while the number of administrative units were decreasing. But if in the future a significant proportion of the learning process is shifted to ITV, then the question of standardized curriculum becomes an issue.

In social and political matters, important changes are often wrought through innumerable small decisions. Such irreversible decisions are being taken now. Will it be in the public interest to trade-off the present dispersion of authority over our educational system for a more efficient "machine"? Until the answer to this question is clearly established as a result of intensive study and thought, the current drift of events poses a very serious threat to traditional local control of our system of mass education.

12 American Media Abroad

The AFRTS

The United States is not only the world's largest user of mass communications; it is also a major supplier. In a field so sensitive that much of the world is prohibited by its governments from hearing or reading another nation's media, America's *private* producers annually sell abroad hundreds of millions of dollars in television programs, including news stories that account for as much as 20 percent of the information provided to most of Western Europe. American television producers supply West European television with nearly as many entertainment programs (other than sports) as does the European Broadcast Union.[1]

In addition to these private sources, about which we will have more to say later, the American government through the Defense and State departments also exports programming. Thousands of American servicemen stationed abroad watch their favorite American television programs each night—minus the commercials. Few of them, however, realize the number of foreign nationals who are also listening to the international system of approximately 300 radio stations and 60 television stations that constitute the Armed Forces Radio and Television Services (AFRTS). In Europe alone, the armed forces radio audience is conservatively estimated at 20 million civilians.

AFRTS had its start on July 4, 1943, in a BBC cellar. Originally designed to serve American Army units in the British Isles during World War II, its responsibilities were expanded as time went on. A reorganization in August of 1967 placed it under the Office of Information of the Armed Forces, which reports to the Assistant Secretary of Defense for Manpower and Reserve Affairs. Its stations are staffed by both civilian and military personnel, with military officers usually serving as station managers. Civilians generally operate the programming and engineering departments.

The content of armed forces radio has been described as reminiscent of American radio before television. It includes packaged interview shows specially recorded in Los Angeles for AFRTS. Most stations, however, use U.S. radio network shows. They are frequently connected directly to the U.S. private networks through shortwave relay. Thus, AFRTS picks up news and sports events at the same time the civilian audiences receive them in the United States. On-the-hour news from major U.S. radio networks is used in rotation and local disc-jockey shows provide all types of music during off-hours.

Television programming, on the other hand, is not carried live from the United States, except on rare occasions. AFRTS TV stations carry standard U.S. fare, videotaped and shipped by air to the armed forces stations. News programs are assembled at each station from film clips flown in and from local sources.

The impact of Armed Forces Radio and Television Services on foreign civilians has not been measured by audience research, since the informing and entertaining of foreign nationals abroad is not an officially recognized objective of the Department of Defense. Clearly, however, the knowledge that there are local audiences does affect programming decisions.

Military Censorship

The experience of AFRTS provides ample evidence that a government-operated communications system finds it virtually impossible to resist the temptation to censor the news. Defense officials say that there is little management of the news and that what there is is justified on grounds of military or national interest. But the facts say otherwise.

In autumn 1969, the 11 radio stations and eight television stations operated by AFRTS in South Vietnam were ordered not to carry accounts of a public statement by South Vietnam's Vice President, Nguyen Cao Ky, announcing a U.S. troop withdrawal. Instead, Americans in Vietnam had to read about it in the local English-language newspapers or the servicemen's own publication, *Stars and Stripes*. Nor did AFRTS listeners hear, until more than a week after it was broadcast and printed widely in the United States, that on one occasion a company of soldiers had refused to fight.

The central operating headquarters for all of AFRTS is in the Washington suburb of Rosslyn. Some orders to kill stories over the entire network have come directly from the nearby Pentagon. One such story concerned the 6,000 sheep killed by lethal nerve gas at the Utah Dugway Proving Ground. AFRTS newsmen in Washington also were told to delete stories concerning speculation that Spain might not renew its treaty permitting U.S. bases there. Ironically, another story killed was a report from a UPI reporter in Saigon telling how AFRTS newsmen had charged, on the air, that their news was being censored.

Although an edict that "the censorship of news stories or broadcasts over such outlets as AFRTS is prohibited" is still in force, there is another Defense Department directive—also still force—that allows information considered sensitive to a host country to be suppressed. Present and former employees of the service say the widest possible interpretation is given to this loophole in order to satisfy news management.

Beyond Censorship

Foreign interest in AFRTS is substantial precisely because it is *not* intended for foreign nationals. The foreign audience wants to know what America is telling its own people about different events. But the American government also operates a system of mass communications *intended* specifically for foreign audiences. These media were designed to meet the needs of an environment most Americans would not even begin to comprehend.

Control over information in the U.S.S.R. had been so stringent that it was a criminal offense to own an unregistered typewriter. The 300-odd million people living in Eastern Europe and the U.S.S.R. were not only denied information that might reflect badly on the government but also information of commonplace events. In the winter of 1989, in the era of *glasnost*, this author visited the Soviet Union and was witness to a Soviet television broadcast on Niagara Falls. In the half-hour broadcast Soviet television never once showed a house, a car, or an American. The program focused exclusively on the water—an amazing feat of editing that prevented the average Russian from obtaining even a glimpse of what life is like abroad.

Indeed, they are even denied information regarding their own laws.[2] The authorities find it easier to violate their laws if the public is ignorant of them. The unlawful exile of Nobel Prize author Alexander Solzhenitsyn was an example of but one of untold violations of the rights of Soviet citizens by their own government. It is the disclosure of these violations in his writings—almost all of which had to be published abroad—that eventually led to his exile. On the other hand, were it not for the fact that his reputation was made known in the U.S.S.R. by foreign broadcast media, his very life would have been at stake for the crime of communicating information.

The American media beamed at Eastern Europe and the U.S.S.R. were not attempting to increase America's popularity. Rather, their purpose was to serve as a surrogate free press for the people living in these closed societies. The motivation was not altruism but a realistic understanding of the *power of information*. The millions spent on this effort was an attempt to limit the freedom of action of these totalitarian regimes. As noted earlier, information is the substance of power. By reducing the state's monopoly on information, these media helped to make the regime answerable—even in a limited way—to public opinion. Indeed, many of the dissidents in Soviet Union are alive today because their names and their alleged offenses were made known throughout Russia by these media.

It was with this in mind that Radio Liberty serialized Solzhenitsyn's book *The Gulag Archipelago* (Harper & Row, 1974) as soon as it was available. The possession of a recording or typed copy of *Gulag* was a criminal offense in the U.S.S.R.—and for a good reason. The book's central theme is a factual account of the violence perpetrated by the Soviet regime on its own people, including the names of persons and details of actual events. Its threat to the regime is an informed public.

The American media involved in these efforts include Radio Free Europe, which is beamed only at Eastern Europe, and Radio Liberty, which is beamed only at the U.S.S.R. The Voice of America also broadcasts into this region, in addition to its broadcasting to the rest of the world.

Since the events of the winter of 1989–90 in Eastern Europe, consideration is being given to unifying these media services. It is now not beyond the realm of possibility that intergovernmental agreements will someday facilitate transmission of television broadcasts across state boundaries. The part of Eastern Europe that borders on the West already receives some TV signals from Scandinavia, West Germany, and Austria. It would, however, be an exaggeration to attribute the collapse of the Russian Empire to outside information. The Communist hegemony within the U.S.S.R. and outside the U.S.S.R. disintegrated by virtue of its own failure to provide a decent life for its people.

The VOA is part of the United States Information Agency (USIA) and accounts for about one-quarter of its budget of $1 billion. The USIA also operates a worldwide network of libraries and public information offices and sponsors international conferences. Many of its efforts are aimed at friendly countries.

Radio Free Europe and Radio Liberty have shared a common budget, of which Radio Liberty generally has received about one-third. RFE listeners number about 30 million people, or nearly half the adult population of Eastern Europe. The size of the audience listening to Radio Liberty is much more difficult to determine. There are fewer Soviet tourists traveling abroad than East Europeans, and Soviet tourists were more likely to be watched when they are abroad and therefore were more reluctant to be interviewed. However, based on the best available information, Radio Liberty estimates that it has reached about 15 percent of the Soviet population during intensive jamming by the authorities.

The size of these audiences does not represent an accurate assessment of their impact. Information in an information-starved country has a way of spreading that makes a simple count of initial listeners a poor basis for evaluation. There has been an instance when these media can take credit for affecting Soviet foreign policy. In 1968, Andrei Sakharov, circulated a memorandum in which he urgently called for bilateral cooperation with the United States on matters of disarmament and environmental control. The SALT treaty and the Environmental Treaty signed five years later are traceable, at least in part, to the stimulus of Sakharov's memorandum. However, this memorandum was not published in Russia but was broadcast back to Russia by Radio Liberty and the VOA.

Despite the importance of these media to the foreign policy of the United States, some Americans propagate the myth that we are improperly interfering in the internal affairs of foreign nations. Among those fostering this view was Senator J. W. Fulbright, when he was Chairman of the Senate Foreign Relations

Committee. However, the act of communicating to foreign nationals is a right that is inscribed in a number of international covenants. Therefore, jamming of foreign radio broadcasts violates Article 19 of the United Nations Charter of Human Rights and Article 48 of the 1965 Montreux International Telecommunications Convention. The Soviet Union is a signatory of both, and takes full advantage of this freedom in *its* overseas broadcasts. Indeed, the Soviets are second only to the United States in exercising that right.

Unofficial Influence: TV Syndication

As far as the free world is concerned, the *official* American media—such as AFRTS and the Voice of America—are relatively unimportant. The flow of *unofficial* (that is, commercial) programming is the principal mode of communication between the United States and the rest of the world. Paradoxically, our contact with the communist countries is limited by their own governments to our official government media. If there were a free flow of information with the communist countries, there would be no need for the USIA, RFE, or Radio Liberty.

The foreign market for American commercial television is considerable. More than 95 percent of all American television network programs are sold in at least one foreign country—most of them during the same season in which they are being shown in the United States.

American television programs are sold to about 100 countries and syndicated television news reaches about 40 countries. Canada, Australia, Japan, and Western Europe are the principal purchasers of American television programs. The prices they pay are based either on the popularity of the programs (number of viewers) or the number of TV sets licensed in the countries that require such licenses. Each half-hour of a popular series sold to Britain, for instance, sells for about $9,000, whereas a half-hour of the same program sold in Panama may bring only $100. Thus, the revenue earned from the export of television programs understates the original cost of production and, inferentially, the number of foreign nationals exposed to American programming.

Initially, U.S. syndication grew at a rapid rate because the desire of other countries for programming outstripped their ability to produce. In addition, U.S. shows are priced to sell at much less than they would cost to be produced abroad. Britain's Independent Television Authority estimated that it could buy a typical U.S. show for one-tenth what it would cost them to produce it. But in recent years, foreign governments, even friendly ones, have been less enthusiastic over the influx of U.S. programming. Britain, Australia, and Canada now prescribe a maximum percentage of programming that may be imported from the U.S. The quota for Australia, for instance, is 14 percent.

United Europe

Following the year 1992, Europe will become, in economic terms, a single nation. It will represent a market with 320 million reasonably prosperous people. This will make it the greatest economic power in the world. It will produce more than the United States and twice as much as Japan. For America's mass-communications industry this change represents both an opportunity and a challenge. The opportunity is obvious, because the growth potential is significant. European officials estimate that the European Community will require at least 120,000 hours of television programming in the 1990s. Neither the Europeans nor the Americans now have enough material to fill all the channels that will be available. Although this market will require an increasing volume of American programming, because it is sold at a fraction of its production cost and would therefore swamp their media, the Community is planning to impose limits on the amount of foreign programming that may be sold in its market.

Restrictions on the importation of programs into Europe could have a dramatic effect on American TV producers. The Motion Picture Association of America estimates that its members sold abroad about $4.4 billion worth of TV programs, films, and home video material in 1988. TV advertising, too, represents a growth market for advertising agencies. Between 1988 and 1992, advertising expenditures in Europe will have grown by 46 percent. In the United States the anticipated growth is 25 percent and in Japan 22 percent.

As a result of these changes and opportunities a major restructuring of companies and industries is underway. Multibillion-dollar sales of American film libraries and the purchase of American advertising agencies by European firms indicates that they are viewing the future with as much aggressiveness as are Americans. While we look for an opportunity to enter Europe they are looking for opportunities to enter America.

Cultural Impact Abroad

It is difficult to assess the impact of television shows exported by America. Some critics in this country worry about the image of America portrayed in some of the more popular programs, which feature crime and violence. Others are concerned over the casual treatment of luxury in America for a world much of which is still full of poverty. Most critics feel that we need to be represented overseas by something more than the cliché formula serials, detective films, and situation comedies. This concern is based on the myth of the public's credulity, a strain that runs through all media-related issues. But a society in which information flows freely is not so easily misled. In Western Europe there is little likelihood that the American fiction shown on Europe's television screens will distort their public's understanding of American realities.

Table 18   U.S. Magazines with Foreign Editions

MAGAZINE	TOTAL FOREIGN CIRCULATION
Reader's Digest	10,946,000
Time	823,000
Popular Mechanics	434,000
Newsweek	229,000

Our Printed Media Abroad

Programs for broadcasting are not the only form of information and entertainment exported by the United States. Approximately 18 million copies of U.S. newspapers and magazines are distributed abroad each month.

U.S. general-interest magazines with international editions, which constitute the bulk of the 18 million copies sold abroad, are ranked in Table 18.

Reader's Digest is by far the most widely circulated magazine in the world. It is published monthly in 30 separate editions.

Table 19   U.S. Magazines: The Circulation Abroad of Regular Domestic Editions

MAGAZINE	TOTAL FOREIGN CIRCULATION	FOREIGN CIRC. AS PERCENTAGE OF TOTAL CIRCULATION
National Geographic	361,000	9.09%
Playboy	325,000	9.75
Ladies' Home Journal	76,000	1.17
McCall's	65,000	0.78
Scientific American	52,000	13.27
Esquire	45,000	5.02
Seventeen	45,000	3.49
House and Garden	42,000	3.01
Popular Photography	40,000	9.51

Table 20   U.S. Newspapers with Foreign Circulation

NEWSPAPER	FOREIGN CIRCULATION
Hablemos (Spanish)	474,000
Herald Tribune: European Ed.	80,000
Journal of Commerce	32,000
Rome Daily American	30,000
Wall Street Journal	20,000
New York Daily News	16,000
Christian Science Monitor	14,000
Miami Herald	12,000
Total	678,000

Both the text and the advertisements take into consideration the cultural sensibilities of particular markets.   Thus, advocacy of birth control would not appear in the Irish edition, nor would the sale of liquor be advocated in editions sent to Moslem countries.

Of U.S. newspapers with overseas circulation, it is surprising that 73 percent of the total circulation is attributable to a U.S. Spanish-language newspaper *Hablemos*, which is little known to most Americans.   Included in the list in Table 20 is a newspaper not published in the U.S., but published specifically for Americans abroad: the *Rome Daily American*.

America's printed material has a smaller overseas audience than American television programs.   Reliable audience figures for U.S. television programs shown abroad are not available, but they are certainly in excess of the 18 million readers who receive U.S. periodicals.   However, if *readership* is a projected at four times the circulation figure, the resulting 72 million is formidable, especially since it is concentrated in Western Europe.

U.S. periodicals are generally received abroad by those whom American advertisers refer to as the "influentials"—people in a position to influence policy and style. Almost 10 percent of the

18-million circulation is accounted for by business, trade, technical, and scholarly journals. These journals necessarily influence
the attitudes of foreign professionals, principally because the
content of these publications is neither frivolous entertainment
nor propaganda, but truly informative and educational. Then,
too, American periodicals have generally reflected American society more realistically than have television programs. In a survey
of TV viewers a few years ago, nearly 60 percent of respondents
did not believe that American life was really like that portrayed
in American TV programs. No magazine would long survive if its
credibility were that low. This statistic also speaks volumes about
the purported gullibility of audiences.

Epilogue

It would have been impossible to plan the American system of mass communications as it is now constituted. The variety of modes, concepts, functions, and audiences that make up the system defies imagination. What is even more startling is that this system evolved from the efforts of thousands of independent decision-makers. Yet, as we have seen, it is a well-balanced and efficient machine.

Entertainment, information, and advertising flow to the American audience in a great variety of print and broadcast packages. The audience is continually surveyed for its opinions and this information results in continual adjustment of media output. No other nation has a mass communications system so finely tuned to the desires of the audience it serves.

As discussed in some detail in this book, there is a clear link between the media's mode of operation and the fact that *no one* in mass communications in the United States is a government employee. The government is excluded, by design, from participating in the operation of the system. This arrangement, however, has from time to time come under pressure from forces outside of government as well as from the government itself. Currently, this is not a matter of major concern.

America's mass communications system is rooted in the soil of commerce, not politics. Indeed, there is not a single *political* network, broadcasting station—or daily newspaper—in the United States. The system is designed to fit into a consumer-oriented economy. Originally, entertainment programs were intended to help sell radio and then, later television receivers. Gradually it evolved that these media were important instruments for the sale of other goods and services. Today they share with newspapers and magazines the important functions of entertaining, informing, and, through advertising, of linking mass production to mass consumption.

We are now on the brink of another major change in mass communications. There are today hundreds of broadband channels in domestic satellites in orbit over the United States. Each channel can carry a video picture or, alternatively, more than a thousand voice conversations. Initially, television will have to follow a circuitous and costly route to reach the nation's homes from these satellites. But the time is not far off when these satellites will be broadcasting directly to the home.

At that point, the process of "creative destruction," discussed earlier, will have again been set in motion, with a significant impact on television broadcasters and the television networks. International use of satellites that broadcast direct to the homes of foreign nationals, much as radio does today is now in its infancy. This could have immense impact on the future of such formerly "closed" societies as Russia and Eastern Europe and possibly even more so with regard to third-world nations.

As we have seen within the United States, there has been a decline in political bossism with the increased development of mass communications. This strongly suggests that the relentless exposure of persons and policies to the glare of public scrutiny exerts a force, not on the audience, but on those whom the audience observes.

It has been fashionable to bemoan the possibility of electing computer-primed "nonentities" to high office simply because of their public charm and the so-called power of the media. However, these observers would do well to look into the past and explain how such charming nonentities as Van Buren, Tyler, Fillmore, Pierce, Hayes, Harrison, and Harding managed to become presidents of the United States. Indeed, it is possible that the relentless public exposure of modern communications would have prevented these lesser lights from attaining high office.

The mass media are like a time machine: They accelerate the process of familiarization. But this familiarity can just as easily breed contempt as popularity. A case in point is the late Senator Joseph McCarthy, who terrorized the federal apparatus but was destroyed by the image he projected on the television screen. Thus, it can be argued that the mass media are image *breakers* with at least as much conviction as the more popular belief that they are image *makers*.

The "power of the media" is a cliché to which reference is almost always made in discussion of this sort. This power has been accepted as real, yet it consists principally of the ability to reach a phenomenal number of people at the same time. If by power one also means the ability to influence, it still remains to be proven that man's ability to direct others has increased because of technology. The existence since the dawn of history of mass movements and totalitarian regimes indicates that political and social ills would still exist, with or without mass communications. One should not forget that Moses, Confucius, Buddha, Jesus, Mohammed, and Marx did not have the benefit of today's sophisticated technology and advertising budgets, yet their points of view and their personalities still command a great deal more attention than that of any of our contemporaries. Perhaps we have forgotten that the key to influencing people is, after all, ideas rather than technology.

Changing the American Mind

Looking at the American scene from about 1970 to the present we see astounding changes taking place in the attitude and behavior of the American people, not merely in public policy but at the most intimate and personal level. It would not be an exaggeration to say that the changes that have taken place in the last three decades have been as sweeping and as significant for the future as has been the collapse of the Soviet Empire. Americans have, in this period, taken formidable strides away from middle-class mores and Judeo-Christian values. The consequences, as we shall see, have been very serious.

How did this come about? Is it attributable in some way to the "power of the media"? Not at all. Mass communications had nothing to do with it. Its root cause, like most fundamental changes in society, derives from an interaction between ideas and events. In this case the idea was freedom and the event was the almost century-long struggle against totalitarianism. For three generations we struggled against the autocracies of Germany, Japan, and the Soviet Union. We defended freedom with our lives and our treasure and generously aided others who wanted their freedom as well.

The problem was that after three generations of conflict, we don't know where to draw the line. We have come to believe that any form of social control, any institution that inhibits our behavior, is opposed to freedom and is therefore an evil.

As the international conflict between the world's two major powers draws to a successful conclusion, social institutions that have served civilization for millennia are being abandoned by many Americans in the name of liberty. The father, the mother, the husband, the family, the police, the teacher, religion, customs, and manners are all falling victim to the call for the elimination of social controls. The Supreme Court, caught up in the spirit of these times, has given this trend its critical support by transforming anti-social behavior, and even selected crimes, into civil rights.

Overt rebellion against social controls and social institutions first found expression in the counterculture of the late 1960s and early 1970s. The youth of that period, raised on the gospel of freedom, found itself facing draft calls to fight for another people's freedom in an unpopular war in Vietnam while witnessing the blacks at home struggling to assert their rights to vote, to be educated, and to be served as equals in public facilities. The youth of that period rebelled. As they themselves expressed it, they "dropped out."

This same American youth who participated in the counterculture by burning the American flag, smoking pot, taking LSD, indulging in uninhibited dress and behavior, taking over the universities, advocating "doing your own thing" and "letting it all hang out"—these youth are today's adults. Today they are the establishment. They are now the gatekeepers of society.

In 1987, a candidate for the Supreme Court had to withdraw his candidacy when it was disclosed that he had broken the law by smoking pot, years before. In 1990, the mayor of Washington, D.C., was accused of drug involvement. One of America's two major wire services, UPI, is now owned by former hippies. Understandably, what was once called bohemia and kept at bay by past gatekeepers the present generation of gatekeepers has allowed to become integrated into conventional society. As a result, what was once bohemian has now become conventional.

The inability to cope properly with the idea of freedom and the contradictions that were prevalent at the time, rather than a childhood spent with Kukla, Fran & Ollie, and Captain Kangaroo, was responsible for triggering the counterculture. Movies, television, and the media in general did not play a serious role in what occurred. The media recorded it, reported it, and integrated it into the entertainment it offered. But the media did not initiate it.

Ironically, these sweeping changes in values and mores took hold of America at the very moment that final victory over political tyranny was at hand. Sad to say, there are indications that the hard-fought battle against totalitarianism may, as a result, end tragically. We can already see the first signs of decay. The quality of American education has declined appreciably as higher education became a "right," even if not earned. Our economic situation is not what it had been or what it could be—because competition and excellence were given a bad name. Serious anti-social behavior has rendered many of our center cities unsafe as we treat violent people with compassion, as if what they do is not their fault, and is, therefore, in some way, their "right."

It was a self-disciplined America that produced the wealth and power that made its institutions so attractive to the less fortunate. Now our former adversaries, Germany and Japan, are becoming ever more successful because they have modeled themselves after the "old" America while the "new" America waddles about in confusion. We are abandoning the standards and values that made America great. We Americans, not our enemies, have shorn the American Samson.

The "melting pot" has disappeared from American nomenclature and given way to "pluralism," not *ethnic pluralism*, which has always been around, but a pluralism based on the rights of the different members of the family. The extended family that had become the nuclear family has now been split into its component parts. A social unit that had heretofore been the bedrock of society has come unglued. The media celebrate this breakdown in situation comedies and family dramas, and the news reports tell of progress in women's rights, children's rights, gay rights, and welfare rights. Aunts, uncles, cousins, and grandparents have all but disappeared from the television image of American life. Drugs, alcoholism, perversion, violence, loneliness, and homelessness are common themes in our entertainment. This is a reflection of what is taking place "out there" in front of the television set.

The mass media perform the task of reporting, recording, and reflecting these changes; they have not initiated them. The indecency that disturbs the Federal Communications Commission is not the result of avaricious advertisers, nor is it the product of the fevered brain of program producers. This indecency is common today in the streets and homes of America. The media merely tell us what is acceptable.

The decline of social and moral values is unrelated to modern technology. Students of history are keenly aware that it has happened before in other societies—well before the advent of mass communications. In every case it marked the decline of those societies.

With the pending economic and political unification of Europe, our adversaries will no longer be the tyrants of the past but the disciplined democracies of the future. This calls for an entirely different approach than that which occupied Americans during a century of hot and cold wars. Is America too exhausted to cope with this unknown future? Are we unable to enjoy the fruits of our hard-won struggle against tyranny? Are we going to continue to "let it all hang out"? Will we join the regimes we defeated "on the scrap heap of history," as our enemies had once forecast? Or will America come to its senses before it is too late?

With skill, luck, and extraordinary effort the situation might be turned around. But it won't be turned around through "sound bites," 30-second "spot" announcements, or by preaching over the mass media. The mass media are designed to inform and to entertain. We cannot look to them for our social salvation. It's not their job and they couldn't accomplish it if they tried.

With time, it will become increasingly evident to the many people who have been misled by the currents of social fashion that they are acting contrary to their own best interests. There can't be very much joy for a child growing up without parental attention and without relatives, for single people to come home to an empty apartment, for young adults to be without children, or for anyone to grow old alone. If the institutions involved in these functions—such as the family, the school, and the church—awaken to their responsibility to educate and to guide, the situation can be returned to its more constructive state. When this happens, the media will be the first to report it. And the character of popular entertainment will reflect it.

Notes

Introduction

1. B. H. Bagdikian, *The Media Monopoly* (Boston: Beacon Press, 1983).

Chapter I

1. Marshall McLuhan, *Understanding the Media: The Extension of Man* (New York: McGraw-Hill, 1964). Harry Crosby, *The McLuhan Explosion* (New York: American Book, 1968). Raymond Rosenthal, *McLuhan: Pro and Con* (New York: Funk & Wagnalls, 1968).
2. *New York Times*, February 18, 1973.
3. Erik Barnouw, *The Image Empire* (New York: Oxford University Press, 1970).
4. *New York Times*, January 26, 1973.

5. FCC Report MM-263 (August 4, 1987).

Chapter 2

1. Series of Senate hearings on the Failing Newspaper Bill (1969–70). Subcommittee on Antitrust and Monopoly, 90th Congress, 1st and 2nd Sessions.
2. Ibid.
3. Jonathan Fenby, *The International News Services* (New York: Schocken Books/Twentieth Century Fund Report, 1986).
4. FCC Annual Financial Summaries.
5. Ibid.
6. Chris Welles, "Can Mass Magazines Survive?", *Columbia Journalism Review* (July/August 1971).
7. Ibid.
8. *Broadcasting Yearbook* (Washington, D.C.: Broadcasting Publications, Inc., 1989).
9. *Gale Directory of Publications* (Detroit: Gale Research Company, 1988).
10. *Time*, March 4, 1974.
11. *Broadcasting Yearbook*, ibid.
12. FCC Release 05693, Table 3 (1973).
13. *Fortune*, April 24, 1989.

Chapter 3

1. *Special Study* (M. H. Seiden & Associates, 1971), FCC Docket 18110. The basic data for this study were obtained from computer tapes through the sources listed below and were coordinated with supplementary up-to-date information available in the trade press. Each media owner was assigned an identification code that permitted the computer to coordinate the data from diverse sources relevant to all of his holdings. Where overlapping ownership existed, ownerships

were combined; e.g., Cowles-Ridder, McCormick-Patterson. Television: American Research Bureau, Inc. Radio: Pulse, Inc. Newspapers: Sinding, Inc. Weeklies: National Newspaper Representatives, Inc. Magazines: American Bureau of Circulation.

Chapter 4

1. The discussion in this chapter draws principally upon the following technical studies published in the years 1988–89 by the National Association of Broadcasters, Washington, D.C. Interpretation of these findings are the authors' alone: "ATV/HDTV" by K. R. Donow; "The Future of Fiber" by S. A. Esty; "Fiber Optic Multipoint Networks" by R. J. Blackburn; "Cable Television" by S. N. Brotman; "Home Video" by S. N. Brotman; and "Personal/Home Audio" by J. D. Abel, R. V. Ducy, and M. R. Fratrik, in *Many Roads Home : The New Electronic Pathways* (NAB, 1988). Also "Broadcasters and Telephone Companies" by Shooshan and Jackson; "Restrictions on Telephone Companies" by Dow, Lohnes and Albertson; and "Cities and States Interest in Telco Video" by Miller and Holbrooke, in *Telco Fibre and Video Market Entry* (NAB, 1989). Also Charles Jackson and Louise Arnheim, *A High Fiber Diet for Television* (NAB, 1988); Marcia De Sonne, *Television Satellite Newsgathering* (NAB, 1988); Marcia De Sonne. *Satellites and Broadcasting* (NAB, 1988). And finally, P. D. Jursek and N. S. Hecht, *Television in Transition* (NAB, 1988).

Chapter 5

1. Newton N. Minow, John Bartlow Martin, and Lee M. Mitchell, *Presidential Television* (New York: Basic Books, 1973), pp. vii–xi.

2. Dale Minor, *The Information War* (New York: Hawthorne Books, 1970), p. 12.
3. Marvin Barrett, ed., *Survey of Broadcast Journalism* (New York : Grosset & Dunlap, 1970), p. 33.
4. *Washington Post*, November 1, 1970.
5. Minow, Martin, and Mitchell, ibid., pp. vii–xi.
6. Seiden, *Special Study*; see notes for Chapter 3.
7. FCC Report on Political Broadcasting (1973).
8. Ibid. In 1972, the presidential campaign accounted for $14.3 million of the $59.3 million spent by all candidates for radio and television (network and station time). Senatorial races accounted for $6.4 million, congressional races for $9.7 million; and all other state and local candidates spent $21.5 million.

Chapter 6

1. E. G. Krasnow and L. D. Longley, *The Politics of Broadcast Regulation* (New York: St. Martin's Press, 1973).
2. *Advertising Age*, January 23, 1989.
3. *Broadcasting*, January 1 and February 12, 1973, p. 24.
4. Ibid., January 8, 1973, p. 16.
5. *The New York Times Magazine*, September 12, 1973.
6. Martin H. Seiden, *Cable Television: U.S.A.* (New York: Praeger Publishers, 1972).
7. B. H. Bagdikian, *The Information Machines* (New York: Harper & Row, 1971).

Chapter 7

1. *Washington Post*, August 16, 1971.
2. Ibid., March 30, 1971.
3. Leo Bogart, "Survey of Foreign Correspondents," *Journalism Quarterly* (Summer 1968).